Organizational Leadership

Organizational Leadership

Knowledge and Skills for K–12 Success

Edited by
Frank S. Del Favero

ROWMAN & LITTLEFIELD
Lanham • Boulder • New York • London

Published by Rowman & Littlefield
An imprint of The Rowman & Littlefield Publishing Group, Inc.
4501 Forbes Boulevard, Suite 200, Lanham, Maryland 20706
www.rowman.com

6 Tinworth Street, London SE11 5AL, United Kingdom

Copyright © 2021 by Frank S. Del Favero

All rights reserved. No part of this book may be reproduced in any form or by any electronic or mechanical means, including information storage and retrieval systems, without written permission from the publisher, except by a reviewer who may quote passages in a review.

British Library Cataloguing in Publication Information Available

Library of Congress Cataloging-in-Publication Data

Names: Del Favero, Frank S., 1948– editor.
Title: Organizational leadership : knowledge and skills for K–12 success / Edited by Frank S. Del Favero.
Description: Lanham : Rowman & Littlefield, [2021] | Includes bibliographical references and index. | Summary: "The purpose of Organizational Leadership: Knowledge and Skills for K–12 Success is to provide the reader with the foundational knowledge and skills that are necessary to become an effective educational leader."—Provided by publisher.
Identifiers: LCCN 2020035496 (print) | LCCN 2020035497 (ebook) | ISBN 9781475839111 (Cloth) | ISBN 9781475839128 (Paperback) | ISBN 9781475839135 (ePub)
Subjects: LCSH: Educational leadership. | Educational accountability. | School improvement programs.
Classification: LCC LB2806 .O6768 2021 (print) | LCC LB2806 (ebook) | DDC 371.2/011—dc23
LC record available at https://lccn.loc.gov/2020035496
LC ebook record available at https://lccn.loc.gov/2020035497

To all students who are currently enrolled in educational leadership preparation programs. In spite of being aware of the many and often overwhelming challenges you will face, the countless hours away from your families that you will spend, and incredible demands your future responsibilities will require of you as future educational leaders, you remain focused and persevere. I admire you for this and wish you success throughout your quest to effectively serve students and staff!

Contents

Acknowledgments	xi
Introduction	xiii
Purpose	xiv
Contents	xiv
Editor's Note	xvi

1 Organizing a Just School in the Age of Accountability — 1
Robert O. Slater, PhD
- Rawls's Two Principles of Justice — 2
- Rawls's First Principle: Differentiating Instruction and Developing the Whole Human Being — 3
- Rawls's Second Principle: Integrating the Three Domains into a Curriculum for All — 4
- Chapter Summary — 5
- Notes — 5

2 The School Improvement Plan — 7
Frank S. Del Favero, PhD
- The SIP: Every School Should Have One — 9
- The Architect Is to the Blueprint as the Principal Is to the School Improvement Plan — 10
- The SIP Process Described — 11
- Continuous Monitoring of the SIP Is Necessary for Success — 14
- A School Improvement Plan Is a Dynamic Plan — 15
- The SIP Format and Elements — 17
- Chapter Summary — 18
- Note — 19

3	Creating a Meaningful School Vision	21
	Nancy P. Autin, PhD	
	School Vision and Beliefs	21
	Establishing a Baseline: Analyzing Current School Data	23
	Data Team Organization and Actions	24
	Identifying Strengths and Opportunities for Improvement	25
	Building Goals through Stakeholder Involvement	26
	Crafting a Revised or New School Vision	28
	Chapter Summary	29
	Notes	29
4	Community Engagement	31
	Tarrah C. Davis, EdD	
	School and Community Relations Communication Plans	31
	Mission, Vision, Goals, Purpose	32
	Contextual Design (School Demographics and Community)	32
	Stakeholders	33
	Needs Assessment	33
	Activities and Strategies	34
	Timeline	35
	Monitoring	35
	Evaluation	36
	School and Community Partnership	36
	Connections with Parents	37
	The Role of Teachers	38
	Community Business Connections	38
	School and Community (Stakeholder Perceptions)	39
	Chapter Summary	39
	Notes	40
5	Inspiring and Leading the Change Process	41
	Erin Stokes, EdD	
	The Chief Change Agent	41
	Chapter Preview	42
	Understanding Change	42
	Readiness for Change	43
	Case Study	44
	Readiness for Reform Matters	44
	School Culture versus School Climate	45
	Case Study	46
	Teacher Efficacy	46
	Initiating the Change	48
	Implementation Case Study	50
	Sustainability	52

Case Study	53
Chapter Summary	54
Notes	56
6 Systems Alignment	**57**
Amanda Shuford Mayeaux, EdD	
Systems Alignment	58
Importance and Significance of Systems Alignment to Federal and State Law	58
Evaluating Alignment to School and District Policies and Procedures	59
Working the Process	60
Importance of Systems Alignment to the Mission and Vision	64
Examining Alignment to the Mission and Vision Statements	65
Next Steps	65
The Alignment Discussion	66
Chapter Summary	68
Notes	68
7 School Leadership and the Law: A Field Guide for Instructional Leaders	**71**
Richard Fossey, JD, and Nathan Roberts, JD, PhD	
Students' Constitutional Rights	72
Constitutional Rights of School Employees	76
Corporal Punishment and Constitutional Concerns	82
Child-Abuse Reporting	83
Title IX: Sexual Harassment of Students by Peers or School Employees	84
Religion and Public Education	85
Family Educational Rights and Privacy Act	86
Chapter Summary	86
References	86
Index	**89**
About the Editor and Contributors	**95**

Acknowledgments

As editor of this book and coordinator of the master's degree program in educational leadership at the University of Louisiana at Lafayette, I would like to express my appreciation of the dedication and collaborative effort displayed by our master's degree faculty in preparing this second book for publication. Our faculty consists of a group of highly qualified and experienced scholars and K–12 practitioners. It will be obvious to the reader that they have been able to merge their extensive knowledge of leadership concepts and theories with their many years of experience as effective K–12 leaders to produce informative and useful chapters addressing the organization of a learning environment.

Introduction

In order to lead an effective school that meets the educational and emotional needs of its students, educational leaders of today have to overcome numerous challenges. Reductions in funding and accountability at both the state and federal levels force school leaders to attempt to accomplish more with less financial support. Many administrators have to deal with teaching staffs that are in constant flux. They often face annual teacher turnover rates of 25 percent or more. Finding qualified professionals to replenish teaching staffs is evolving into an almost impossible task. This is because fewer and fewer people are entering the teaching profession. The low rate of compensation and society's general lack of respect for education and educators deter individuals from entering the teaching profession.

As a result, human resources directors and principals often find themselves desperately searching for qualified and certified individuals to fill vacancies in their teaching staffs. It is not uncommon to find schools that start the academic year with individuals assigned to teaching positions who lack proper training and licensure. All these conditions have a negative impact on school culture and climate and on the quality of teaching and learning.

The home environment our students face greatly influences their attitudes and behavior. A brief examination of a school's student demographics often shows high percentages of students living in single-parent households, or living with grandparents. Homelessness and poverty are also issues that impact education and require social service resources that are beyond the academic services and support that schools traditionally provided in the past.

In spite of these challenges, educational leaders are held accountable for creating and maintaining an environment that is conducive to teaching and learning. Our students both deserve and have a right to attend school that has an environment where they can flourish and learn and become contributing members of society. In order to face and overcome these challenges, today's educational leaders must develop and refine the knowledge and skills that are associated with organizing and maintaining an effective learning environment while at the same time addressing the social and emotional needs of their students.

This book, *Organizational Leadership: Knowledge and Skills for K–12 Success*, provides the reader with meaningful information that can be used by educational leaders to overcome these challenges. The topics presented here address many of the essential elements involved in organizing a school environment that supports teaching and learning.

PURPOSE

The purpose of *Organizational Leadership: Knowledge and Skills for K–12 Success*, like its companion, *Instructional Leadership: Knowledge and Skills for K–12 Success*, is to serve as a handbook and/or reference for those currently serving in a position as school leader as well as for those who aspire to become educational leaders.

Central office administrators can use the topics presented in this book to guide professional development of the administrative staff. A building-level administrator can share this book with his or her school's leadership team to assist team members as they further develop and refine their knowledge of what it takes to organize and lead an educational institution. Educational leadership preparation programs can use both *Organizational Leadership* and its companion *Instructional Leadership* as textbooks.

CONTENTS

While *Instructional Leadership: Knowledge and Skills for K–12 Success* targets knowledge and skills directly associated with instruction, this book, *Organizational Leadership: Knowledge and Skills for K–12 Success*, focuses on knowledge and skills relating to the organizational concepts and processes involved in leading and oversight of K–12 schools.

Organizational Leadership: Knowledge and Skills for K–12 Success contains seven chapters, each presenting useful information that school leaders at both the building and central office levels can refer to as they carry out their responsibilities.

Chapter 1, "Organizing a Just School in the Age of Accountability," presents John Rawls's concept of justice, which states that all students have freedom to learn and freedom to learn in a manner that best suits the learning style of the student. The chapter also discusses the roles that each of the domains of knowing plays in the teaching and learning process. Educators must realize that learning involves more than just the cognitive domain and that the attributes of the affective and psychomotor domains must be merged with it.

The process for developing a school improvement plan (SIP) is discussed in chapter 2. In this chapter, the reader will learn that a SIP is a necessary element that guides the school improvement process. The reader will also learn that the SIP is a dynamic document that impacts students, parents, teachers, and noninstructional staff that continually evolves as a result of an ongoing monitoring process.

Chapter 3 defines the meaning and purpose of a school vision. This chapter illustrates how to use data to guide the process of creating a school vision. The reader will learn that a school vision is more than a simple statement of which school stakeholders are unaware; the school vision represents the driving force and statement that defines the desired outcomes of the school.

The fourth chapter of this book addresses the topic of community engagement and focuses on how schools should develop communication plans to effectively communicate with the people in the communities they serve. An effective school communication plan is the vehicle by which a school can establish, maintain, and strengthen connections between a school and its community stakeholders.

Chapter 5, "Inspiring and Leading the Change Process," deals with the change process, school climate and culture, and teacher efficacy. This chapter also presents the challenges an educational leader may face in effecting change.

In the sixth chapter, "Systems Alignment," the reader will learn about the need to align district- and building-level policies with state and federal rules and regulations. While this topic may not sound exciting, systems alignment is a critical element in the process of organizing the learning environment. Systems alignment is the process of making certain that a school's organizational structure meets its legal responsibilities with regard to students and staff at both the state and federal levels.

In chapter 7, "School Leadership and the Law: A Field Guide for Instructional Leaders," important topics such as constitutional rights of students and employees, free speech, religion, and special education are discussed. Educational leaders must be aware of and knowledgeable of laws involving students and staff. This is especially true as we find ourselves living in a litigious society.

EDITOR'S NOTE

This book, *Organizational Leadership: Knowledge and Skills for K–12 Success*, and its companion, *Instructional Leadership: Knowledge and Skills for K–12 Success*, are the result of extensive collaboration among the faculty of the master of educational leadership degree program at the University of Louisiana at Lafayette, College of Education, Department of Educational Foundations and Leadership.

Chapter One

Organizing a Just School in the Age of Accountability

Robert O. Slater, PhD

Few educational leaders would probably dispute the proposition that our K–12 schools ought to be more just than they are, that we should organize schooling to help students not only to learn but do so as they best can, and that we should eliminate the inequalities that prevent them from learning up to their potential. But while most school principals and teachers would agree with this, they might also feel that the demands of accountability—standards and testing—prevent many of the decisions that would shape schools and instruction in ways more consistent with these preferences.

School leaders who believe that accountability prevents them from making schools and schooling more just probably do so because they have not been given a clear enough picture of what the basic principles of justice in a democratic society are. What they know about justice they get by way of discussions of "social justice," one of the most prominent buzzwords in educational administration these days.

However, most of the work on "social justice," at least that which applies to schools and schooling, focuses mainly on "demarginalization," an important part of justice but by no means the whole of it. Demarginalization focuses on students of color and students with different sexual identities, students who are said to be marginalized, that is, pushed to the side of the schooling process and left out of or denied important learning experiences that other more privileged students have. Demarginalization is making sure that these and other students who are marginalized are moved from the periphery back to the center of schooling and get the best instruction available.

The demarginalization scholarship in the social justice educational leadership literature is not completely off the mark. It does address one aspect of the problem of justice, namely, that bearing on inequality. Marginalization is unjust because it promotes inequality in education by creating a situation where some students get more or better schooling while others get less or worse but where everybody ought to be getting an equal amount of the best quality available. So, correcting marginalization by demarginalizing restores some justice to the schooling process because it recognizes and eliminates some inequality.

However, while demarginalization promotes a measure of justice in schools, it does not give school leaders the "viewing equipment" they need to see the organizational infrastructure of injustice in the schools. It focuses attention on the most egregious instances of injustice. While the elimination of these cases is certainly desirable, the risk is that they will reappear after a time because the underlying organizational structures that give rise to and support them have not themselves been removed. They have not been removed in many cases simply because their connection to inequality is not immediately apparent. School leaders need a broader and deeper understanding of justice to "see" them.

Viewing justice in education as demarginalization takes an approach to justice that is narrower than that found in some of the best contemporary works on the subject, in, for example, John Rawls's *A Theory of Justice*.[1] A summary of Rawls's theory might help to sharpen the mind's eye of those whose business it is to design and organize K–12 schooling.

RAWLS'S TWO PRINCIPLES OF JUSTICE

John Rawls, said to be the most important normative political philosopher of the twentieth century, published *A Theory of Justice* in 1971.[2] The book has since become the go-to guide for judging policy and policy making in and for a liberal democratic society. The edition I am going to use in what follows was published in 1999.[3]

The core of Rawls's theory involves two principles of justice, one having to do with freedom and the other with equality. Freedom and equality are two main pillars of a democratic society, and such a society's constituent institutions—whether they be economic, cultural, or educational—ought to conform to the basic principles of the society as a whole. Rawls's two principles are as follows:

> First: each person is to have an equal right to the most extensive scheme of equal basic liberties compatible with a similar scheme of liberties for others.

Second: social and economic inequalities are to be arranged so that they are both (a) reasonably expected to be to everyone's advantage, and (b) attached to positions and offices open to all.[4]

RAWLS'S FIRST PRINCIPLE: DIFFERENTIATING INSTRUCTION AND DEVELOPING THE WHOLE HUMAN BEING

Applying Rawls's first principle to K–12 schools, we can say that each student is to have an equal right to the most extensive scheme of equal basic liberties compatible with a similar scheme of liberties for other students and, further, that the most extensive scheme of basic liberties in the context of education must include not only the freedom to learn but the freedom to do so as one learns best. A just school, therefore, must be one that works to accommodate different ways or "styles" of learning, one that provides differentiated instruction.

Carol Ann Tomlinson provides a useful definition of differentiated instruction:

> Kids of the same age aren't all alike when it comes to learning any more than they are alike in terms of size, hobbies, personality, or food preferences. Kids do have many things in common, because they are human beings and because they are all young people, but they also have important differences. . . . At its most basic level, differentiating instruction means "shaking up" what goes on in the classroom so that students have multiple options for taking in information, making sense of ideas, and expressing what they learn. In other words, a differentiated classroom provides different avenues to acquiring content, to processing or making sense of ideas, and to developing products so that each student can learn effectively.[5]

Tomlinson's definition of differentiated instruction also reminds us that education is first and foremost about human beings. Being about human beings and their development, a just education cannot aim to produce incomplete and partial human beings but must work toward the fulfillment of their human potential, their capacity to be fully human. But if the aim of a just education is the full and complete development of human beings, then differentiated instruction should also strive for not only cognitive development but also the development of the affective and psychomotor domains as well.

In other words, to organize a school in the interest of justice, one would need to organize for the development of the *whole* human being and not just selected aspects. It is unjust, therefore, to exaggerate cognitive development at the expense of the other domains because it is, in effect, failing to enable human beings to make themselves more complete.

Educators have long recognized that the cognitive domain is only one of three domains that comprise the complete human being. Nonetheless, and perhaps largely because of the pressures of accountability, the affective and psychomotor domains have been given much less attention than the cognitive.

Another reason that there has been less attention paid to the development of the affective and psychomotor domains has perhaps to do with the rather narrow ways in which they have been interpreted. The psychomotor domain, for example, is usually thought of mainly as physical activity. Within the context of schooling, this has naturally led educators to emphasize physical and vocational education.

But seeing this domain simply in terms of physical activity is a mistake, for it has to do not with sheer physical activity but with procedural knowledge, the kind of know-how that is characteristic of good career education. Psychomotor development entails the development of our capacity to do things, our know-how.

Where the psychomotor domain has traditionally been too narrowly construed, the affective domain suffers from the opposite tendency; it has been too broadly interpreted as "socioemotional development." This understanding tends to obscure the affective domain's most important point, namely, that it has mainly to do with character and character development.

RAWLS'S SECOND PRINCIPLE: INTEGRATING THE THREE DOMAINS INTO A CURRICULUM FOR ALL

However, a just school would not only give *all* students access to the development of all three domains, but it would also need to integrate the three domains into each subject matter. This is because our experience with the "comprehensive" high school, a brainchild of James B. Conant, showed that while the comprehensive school made all three domains accessible to all students, students were in fact segregated according to whether they planned to go to college or were encouraged to pursue a practical career.[6]

The three domains were offered in the comprehensive curriculum but not to all. The stigma attached to career or, as it was called at the time, "vocational" education, caused college-bound students to self-select out of psychomotor-oriented classes, and voc-ed students were discouraged or even not allowed to enroll in the college-prep tracks.

The way that the comprehensive high school played out in practice violated Rawls's second principle. Students became in effect separated into different categories and the categories were given differentiated instruction, but the differentiation was not to the advantage of all, as Rawls's second principle would have it. Nor was it easy for students to move back and forth from one track to the other, as Rawls's principle stipulates they should be able to do. It was an unjust organization that ended up benefiting the college bound more than the career education students as the economy in the U.S. grew to favor the college educated and corporate America shifted to foreign and cheaper labor.

CHAPTER SUMMARY

In a society committed to the democratic ideal as its main organizing principle, Rawls's two principles of justice should be among the criteria always kept in mind by leaders and managers as they go about the business of mobilizing and organizing the collective will and effort of those with whom they work. This point applies especially to school principals and managers whose business it is to prepare students to live and work in a democratic society committed to the values of freedom and equality.

If students are to learn to appreciate these two values, they need to experience them in the course of their schooling. They can only do so if they are permitted not only to learn but to learn as they best can, in ways that are most effective for them. This means differentiated instruction. But if instruction is to be truly differentiated, then it cannot focus solely on the development of the cognitive domain at the expense of the other two. Instruction must include experience with the affective and psychomotor aspects of the human being as well, and must do so not in a piecemeal way but in an integrated fashion for all students.

What does this mean in practice and in terms of how instruction and schooling should be organized? There is likely no single answer to this question, but a good start on it would have instruction and organization that pays close attention to (a) having students work in small inquiry-creativity teams, (b) to do standards-guided research, (c) for the purpose of learning how to produce or create some product—digital, visual, physical, process, or otherwise, (d) on a tight, perhaps weekly schedule, (d) and then having them evaluate, as a class (perhaps at the end of each week) their own work and its product(s), (e) in addition to having the teachers' feedback.

NOTES

1. John Rawls, *A Theory of Justice*, 2nd ed. (Cambridge, MA: Harvard University Press, 1999).
2. William Kymlicka, *Contemporary Political Philosophy: An Introduction* (Oxford: Clarendon, 1990).
3. Rawls, *A Theory of Justice*.
4. Rawls, *A Theory of Justice*, 53.
5. Carol Ann Tomlinson, *How to Differentiate Instruction in Academically Diverse Classrooms*, 3rd ed. (Alexandria, VA: ASCD), 1.
6. William Wraga, "The Comprehensive High School in the United States: A Historical Perspective" (paper presented at the annual meeting of the American Educational Research

Association, New Orleans, LA, April 24–28, 2000), https://files.eric.ed.gov/fulltext/ED443170.pdf.

Chapter Two

The School Improvement Plan

Frank S. Del Favero, PhD

In this chapter we will discuss and define the concept of a school improvement plan (SIP). After reading this chapter, the reader will gain a better understanding of the purpose and content of an effective school improvement plan and the influential role it plays in refining the way an organization functions. The reader will also become aware of why every school, regardless of its performance scores, should develop and implement a school improvement plan. School leaders will realize that once all stakeholders acquire an understanding of the concept of a school improvement plan, the process of "selling" the concept to stakeholders and developing a viable school improvement plan becomes much more meaningful and efficient.

The idea of an improvement plan is neither new nor radical. A common characteristic among successful public, private, for-profit, and nonprofit organizations is their ongoing practice of self-assessment that includes the regular evaluation of staff and processes, and the continual measurement and analysis of the quality and effectiveness of the goods or services that they provide. In addition, successful organizations have in place an improvement process that measures and analyzes data to identify areas of success and areas of concern, sets realistic measurable goals, and lastly, implements and monitors the effectiveness of improvement strategies.

Schools, unlike a majority of other organizations, do not produce goods or provide services in the traditional sense. Instead, the goal of schools is to educate their students. The tasks and responsibilities placed on our educational system are varied. During the twelve to sixteen years that are traditionally devoted to knowledge and skill development, a school also has the responsibility to address its students' physical and emotional needs. From an affective perspective, a school needs to foster in its students an appreciation for lifelong learning and to instill attitudes and a work ethic that form the basis for students' future success as productive and contributing members of a democratic society.

These are by no means small tasks and simple challenges for our educational system. In fact, the future condition of our society is tightly woven to the quality of the students prepared by our educational institutions. It is therefore critical that we have a clear vision of the attitudes, knowledge, and skills our students should possess as they complete their schooling and enter society as young adults.

In order to effectively meet the educational needs of students, educators must constantly monitor student performance data both formatively (as the academic year progresses) and summatively (at the very end of the academic year). We must note that continuous monitoring/evaluation of data is not limited to academic performance data alone. The results of any SIP intervention strategies addressing school process or that impact stakeholder perceptions need to be monitored as well. The evaluation of these data should take place throughout the school year and can be used to measure the effectiveness of the SIP intervention strategies.

Formative evaluation of data allows the SIP team to determine the extent that SIP intervention strategies in effect actually address the identified areas of concern and have a positive impact on student learning, school process, school climate, or whatever areas of concern targeted by the SIP. The SIP team can also use formative data as the basis for making any midcourse modifications it may deem necessary.

Summative evaluation of the various data types, on the other hand, takes place as soon as the year-end data are available. Examples of the variety of data types of year-end data include standardized test scores, report card and end-of-course test scores, graduation rates, attendance rates, student discipline and attendance data, master schedule, and stakeholder perceptions. The analysis of the various data types (demographic, school process, perception, and student performance data) must function as the foundation on which the modification or implementation of new instructional strategies, curricula, and school processes as outlined in the SIP are based.

The data analysis process makes up the backbone of the SIP process. The process can be summarized in the following six sequential steps:

1. Data analysis is initially used to identify areas of success and areas of concern.
2. Once an area of concern is identified, root cause analysis (RCA) is employed to discover the original factor(s) that allowed the problem area to manifest itself.
3. Through data-based decision-making, proven research-based strategies and interventions addressing the root cause(s) of the area(s) of concern are identified and implemented.

4. Data representing the effects of the SIP strategies and interventions are regularly collected throughout the school year.
5. The ongoing (i.e., formative) evaluation of these data serves to monitor the progress and effectiveness of the implemented strategies and interventions. This provides the SIP team with the opportunity to make any appropriate modifications to the interventions or strategies.
6. The sixth and final step of data analysis involves end-of-year (i.e., summative) data. The SIP team analyzes pertinent end-of-year data in order to determine if the goals and objectives laid out in the SIP were achieved. These determinations then form the basis for next year's SIP.

THE SIP: EVERY SCHOOL SHOULD HAVE ONE

With the advent of the No Child Left Behind Act (NCLB), school accountability became a priority among educators and policy makers. This is evidenced by the fact that NCLB required schools that did not reach adequate yearly progress (AYP) goals to produce SIPs. Under No Child Left Behind and in many states, only those schools that are not meeting the adequate yearly progress (AYP) are required to create a school improvement plan. There are, however, some states and school districts that mandate the creation of a SIP regardless of the academic performance of a school's students. It is my opinion, that all schools, regardless of their academic standing, should create a SIP.

For schools with poor student performance scores, or student academic performance gaps based on gender, socioeconomic status, ethnicity, educational classification, English language proficiency, high dropout rates, low graduation rates, or high teacher turnover rates, the reasons for creating a SIP are obvious. For schools that are making AYP, the administration and instructional staff should still continue to strive toward "perfection."

I am certain that even schools meeting AYP requirements can identify specific areas needing "fine-tuning" in order to bring about additional improvement. Some examples that successful schools could identify as areas that could be improved include increasing the percentage of graduating students who apply and are accepted for admission to upper-tier four-year colleges and universities, increasing the number and availability of college credit–bearing courses offered to the school's junior and senior students, or providing students with the opportunity to earn an International Baccalaureate degree.

One must also not forget the need and importance of preparing the students who decide not to enter postsecondary education to have the skills and attitudes to become productive members of the workforce in a career of their own choosing and for which their K–12 schools prepared them.

The creation and implementation of a SIP should not be seen as an indicator of failure or poor performance. The creation and implementation of a SIP should be viewed for what it is: the blueprint that is based on a vision of what the school's stakeholders want it to become and accomplish and, at the same time, sets meaningful, measurable goals and the way to achieve them. "We are *good* because we want to be *better*" would be an appropriate catchphrase for all schools as they carry out the process of creating and implementing a SIP.

THE ARCHITECT IS TO THE BLUEPRINT AS THE PRINCIPAL IS TO THE SCHOOL IMPROVEMENT PLAN

I like to use analogies whenever introducing or discussing concepts with students and colleagues. For this book, I have chosen to present and describe the concept of a school improvement plan through the use of an analogy dealing with the design and construction of a house. In this analogy, the building principal acts as the architect and the blueprints represent the school improvement plan.

Before designing a house, an architect develops a conceptual idea of the type of house he or she will design, how it will be used, the number and size of the various rooms and bathrooms, and so forth. All of this is based on the particular needs and desires of the client. The architect takes all of this into consideration as she draws up the blueprint for the construction of a house. It is important to note that the architect incorporates within the design recognized and proven aesthetic and structural elements and construction processes that will meet the particular needs of the client.

The principal plays a similar role in developing an improvement plan for her school. The conceptual idea of what her school should be like (the school's vision statement) is based on input from the stakeholders of the school, which include parents, students, instructional and noninstructional staff, and community members. The school's vision statement is simply a brief statement describing the characteristics of the school as it serves the educational, social, and emotional needs of its students (we discuss the development of a school vision statement in greater detail in chapter 3). The school's vision statement serves as the conceptual framework describing the manner in which a school functions and the service it offers its students and is the foundation on which the SIP rests.

Like an architect who designs and draws the blueprints that will be used to define the use and physical characteristics of a building and guide the actual construction process, a building principal works with her stakeholders/

clients to develop a school improvement plan that will serve as a blueprint to help the school evolve into the entity that everyone would like the school to become. Also, like the architect's blueprint, the school improvement plan defines the characteristics of the changes and improvements to the school organization.

The SIP is the "blueprint" that guides the conceptual reconstruction of the school. For all the stakeholders in the school, it is a formal commitment to introduce and implement change with the goal of improving the manner in which the school serves its students and thereby creates a positive impact on the targeted areas of student performance. The school improvement plan process, if properly followed, will result in observable and measurable gains for the clients/students in the areas targeted by the SIP.

THE SIP PROCESS DESCRIBED

The SIP process involves many elements that all must mesh with each other and work together to establish an appropriate and effective SIP.

- First and foremost, in my opinion, is the fact that the SIP must be *based on the school vision*. Essentially, the school vision is a statement that describes what the school's stakeholders would like the school to be in regard to the manner in which it serves its students. An effective and meaningful SIP provides the means to bring about the change that is necessary to make the school vision a reality.
- The next important element necessary for creating a SIP involves the establishment of a collaborative team representing all stakeholders. The chief benefit of the creation of a collaborative team representing all stakeholders is that everyone (parents, students, instructional and noninstructional staffs, and community members) associated with the school either directly or indirectly has the opportunity to provide his or her opinions and ideas while taking part in the SIP process. Collaboration creates and reinforces an atmosphere of *community* and *ownership* where stakeholders are actively involved in the process and feel responsible for the development, implementation, monitoring, and modifications to the SIP.
- A careful detailed *analysis of various types of data* (demographic, performance, school process, and perception data) should be performed. Among other things such as age, grade level, and so forth, demographic data provide information regarding ethnicity, gender, socioeconomic status, language proficiency, attendance, and educational classification of students. Performance data include, for example, academic scores from report cards, teacher-generated assessments, and standardized test scores. School process data provide information regarding how school processes

are carried out and include information such as the master schedule and student behavior. Perception data are an information source that describes what people associated with the school actually believe represents reality at the school. In all, the purpose of data analysis is to uncover empirical evidence that identifies areas of success as well as areas that may need attention.

- Once the data analysis uncovers and identifies areas of concern, the next step in the SIP process involves *root cause analysis (RCA)*, which is a process whose purpose is to find the actual source/cause of the problem.[1] For example, poor performance scores on a summative measure of student achievement on a standardized assessment in mathematics may drive teachers and administrators (using "gut" feelings and assumptions) to initiate tutoring programs to further develop and refine students' math skills, purchase additional math instructional materials, or consider the purchase of a new textbook series, and so on. Using the RCA process may indicate that none of this is necessary because the process discovered, by digging past failing and passing percentages, that students tended to do poorly on the word problems found on the assessments. The RCA process in this example determined that the root cause of low math academic performance scores rests on the fact that the students' poor reading skills and inability to understand and solve mathematical word problems were the cause of the low scores. In this example, the SIP team would initiate processes that focus on improving and refining math students' reading comprehension and interpretative skills. The math teachers would be asked to target the development of knowledge and skills necessary to solve word problems. As soon as the root cause of poor math scores is discovered, the SIP team can move to the next step in the school improvement process.
- The *creation of a hypothesis* by the SIP team is the next step in the school improvement process. A hypothesis is formulated based on the SIP collaborative team's use of the RCA process that involves the interpretation of the various types of data as mentioned above. The hypothesis defines the "problem(s)" that the SIP collaborative team feels negatively impacts the instructional effectiveness, which in turn lowers the rate of academic success.
- The hypothesis is used to *identify appropriate and effective research-based school improvement strategies*. Using basic search strategies, the SIP team can electronically search the many available digital databases of educational journals and other publications to create a literature review. There are vast collections of articles and reports containing proven, research-based instructional strategies and interventions available on the World Wide Web. The SIP team would then use its literature review to select and implement the most appropriate strategies that would result in

improvements and change in the areas identified as needing specific interventions, for example: reading and word problem–solving skills.
- After having identified areas of concern through RCA and finding appropriate research-based interventions, the next task of the SIP collaborative team is to *set reasonable, achievable, and measurable goals and objectives*. The school's stakeholders will perceive the SIP's goals and objectives as reasonable and achievable if they believe that they have or will develop the capacity to attain them. They also come to realize that the goals and objectives are reasonable and achievable when they see that the goals are not set so low as to make a mockery of the entire process nor are the goals set so high that reaching them becomes an impossible and unreasonable expectation. For the stakeholders, setting goals either too low or unrealistically too high makes the creation of a sense of ownership in the SIP as well as its desired outcomes an impossible task. The result is a lack of wholehearted, enthusiastic implementation of the interventions outlined in the SIP. Lacking a sense of ownership by stakeholders in the SIP, even the best plan is doomed to fail. Lastly, goals and objectives must be established in a manner that clearly states and defines the desired outcomes. Goals and objectives have to be measurable. If, for example, one of the SIP hypotheses is that poor attendance is having a detrimental effect on sixth-grade standardized test scores in math, then an appropriate reasonable, attainable, and measurable goal would be to improve the rate of average daily attendance among students in the sixth grade from 89.4 percent to 96.4 percent over a three-year period by at least 3 percent the first year and by at least 2 percent in each of the subsequent years.
- *The success of the SIP hinges entirely upon the extent that all stakeholders are aware of the SIP's purpose and goals.* Creating the most thorough, well-researched, and innovative SIP is absolutely meaningless unless the plan is accepted on a school-wide basis with the full participation of everyone. Unless all of the school's stakeholders are fully aware of the SIP and the impact that their participation and the extent that they carry out their assigned roles and responsibilities have in determining the success or failure of the SIP, the SIP will not achieve its stated goals and objectives. Everyone in the school (students; parents; community members; and instructional, noninstructional, and administrative staffs) must develop a sense of responsibility and a feeling of ownership in the SIP. This will ensure school-wide participation and the implementation of the success-building strategies identified by the SIP.

CONTINUOUS MONITORING OF THE SIP IS NECESSARY FOR SUCCESS

As noted in the bullets above, school-wide implementation of SIP strategies is a key step toward meeting the goals and objectives established by the SIP process. Unfortunately. in many instances, after the SIP is created and the implementation of its requisite interventions and strategies are announced, little to nothing is done to ensure that their implementation is universal, consistent, and ongoing. For there to be any chance that the SIP-initiated strategies and interventions attain their intended levels of success, *continual monitoring of the extent that SIP strategies and interventions are implemented* is necessary.

School administrators are generally responsible for oversight and evaluation of instructional and noninstructional staffs. Because of this, it becomes the building administrators' responsibility to continually monitor the extent and quality of implementation of SIP interventions and strategies. This can be accomplished through daily observations and "walk-throughs" in the school hallways, assembly areas, and classrooms.

In addition to continually monitoring the extent and quality of implementation of the SIP's identified strategies and interventions, there must also *be ongoing monitoring and evaluation of the effectiveness of school improvement strategies themselves* . For example, if the goal of one of the SIP interventions is to increase both teacher and student time-on-task by developing and refining teachers' classroom management skills, then during observations and classroom walk-throughs building administrators would expect to see teachers and students engaged in productive and meaningful learning activities and much less time involved in addressing student behavior and "housekeeping" issues.

Careful analysis and monitoring of the evaluation and walk-through data can determine whether the new classroom management strategies are effective. Data-based conclusions can be drawn to determine the quality and extent of implementation of newly acquired classroom management strategies. If data analysis and monitoring suggest that there exists an improvement that matches or exceeds SIP goals and objectives regarding time-on-task, then no modifications to the SIP are necessary. Should it be determined that, on a school-wide basis, the interventions are making a smaller than expected impact on time-on-task, then minor modifications can be made to the SIP.

Continual monitoring of SIP interventions could also identify individual teachers who are not effectively implementing and applying SIP strategies. These identified teachers can then be referred for further, more individualized training and supervision. In short, continual monitoring and data analysis provide school leaders with opportunities to regularly and continually make any necessary adjustments to the school improvement plan throughout the academic year.

A SCHOOL IMPROVEMENT PLAN IS A DYNAMIC PLAN

Unfortunately, many schools create school improvement plans because they are mandated by state law or required by local school board policy. Oftentimes individuals in leadership positions are neither knowledgeable of the school improvement process nor aware of the possible benefits of a well-designed, implemented, and monitored SIP. These individuals go on to create the mandated SIPs simply because they have to. The plans are created so that they can be filed and sent to the proper persons or agencies solely for the purpose of satisfying requirements and mandates.

In these instances, there is relatively little effort to create and implement a SIP to bring about change and improvement in the manner in which a school meets the educational needs of its students. These plans are generally created by an individual or small group of well-meaning individuals who are unwilling to "burden" others with the task of creating a SIP for their school. They ignore and do not seek input from stakeholders. School improvement plans created under these conditions are rarely implemented, monitored, or modified.

In the few cases where they are implemented, they are by their nature static documents that involve little, if any, "ownership" by the stakeholders. The plans developed in such an environment are, for the most part "dead," static documents that reside on classroom shelves or in filing cabinets where they lie unused and collecting dust until they are disposed of in order to make room for the new SIP the following year. In these schools, the SIP is looked upon as simply another mandated task that is placed upon school leaders.

Here are characteristics of a properly contrived SIP:

1. Developed with input and collaboration from all stakeholders and SIP team members
2. Based on a purposeful collection of data
3. Coupled with a careful and detailed analysis of various data types
4. Guided by decisions based on the analysis of data
5. Focused on examining valid and reliable scientific research to uncover solutions addressing areas of concern
6. Based on realistic, attainable, and measurable goals
7. Continuously monitored and modified as appropriate

It is these characteristics that make the SIP a "living," dynamic document that not only meets local and statewide mandates, but also serves as the

Figure 2.1. The school improvement plan (SIP) process. *Courtesy of the author*

blueprint that will guide and assist a school and its stakeholders as they modify and build new programs and processes that will better serve the educational and emotional needs of the students. School leaders who treat the SIP as a living, dynamic document make certain that it is placed in the hands of the appropriate stakeholders.

They also regularly refer to the SIP throughout the school year and constantly remind their staffs of the goals and objectives that are set forth in the SIP. These leaders also hold their staffs accountable for reaching the goals and objectives identified in the SIP. The educational leaders in schools having dynamic SIPs routinely work to ensure that strategies and interventions found in the plan are fully implemented while at the same time monitor the quality of the implementation. They make certain that timelines established in the SIP are followed and met. School leaders also supervise individuals to ascertain that they are addressing the tasks and responsibilities assigned to them in the SIP.

THE SIP FORMAT AND ELEMENTS

Thus far, the discussion has focused on the SIP process and its purpose. In this last section of this chapter, I would like to talk about the content elements and format of SIP documents. Many states have electronic templates available online for download by school officials. The use of these templates ensures uniformity and consistency among the SIP documents submitted by various schools and school districts to their respective state's Department of Education. More importantly, these electronic SIP templates serve as a checkoff list that school improvement teams can use as they prepare and record information for their SIPs.

The reader may wish to review and/or download examples of school improvement plans from all over the country, or more specifically, SIP documents that may be available in one's respective state. The reader can do this by doing an internet search for "school improvement plans."

Although one may find several variations of SIP templates online, for the most part, they contain the following elements:

- A cover page that includes the name of the school and school district, as well as the names and signatures of the building principal and school superintendent
- A description of the type of school (charter, public, Title I, grade configuration, etc.)
- School vision and mission statements
- A list of both instructional and noninstructional staff positions and numbers in each position

- A list of school improvement team members, their positions, and signatures
- A list of the educational programs and services offered at the school
- School performance scores and any other measures that are included in the calculations used to determine a school's overall performance rating. These data may include, in addition to standardized test scores:
  - Teacher retention rates
  - Student dropout rates
  - Graduation rates
  - Average daily attendance
  - Student cohort data relating to the time it takes for students to graduate
  - Student discipline data such as incidents of student violence, in- and out-of-school-suspension rates
- Data analyses that indicate areas of success and areas of concern. These data would include a description of the data and the data source(s).
- A list of research-based strategies and interventions that would be used to target the identified areas of concern
- A list of goals and objectives that are observable and measurable
- An action plan that shows the following:
  - Specific strategies and interventions to address the goals and objectives for each target area
  - A timeline showing the dates the various components of the interventions are to be implemented
  - The person(s) responsible for the implementation and oversight of the planned interventions
  - The manner by which the effectiveness of the interventions in achieving the SIP's objectives are to be measured

CHAPTER SUMMARY

In this chapter, the reader has learned that the creation of a school improvement plan (SIP) is an important and necessary step in the school improvement process. The creation, implementation, and monitoring of a SIP is an ongoing and dynamic process that plays an essential role in the change process. All schools, whether high or low performing, should create and implement a SIP. The reader has also learned that it is important to include all the stakeholders in the formation of a SIP.

Specifically, the building principal acts as facilitator for the school leadership team as it constructs the SIP. The school improvement team gathers input from the instructional staff, interprets it, and includes the findings in the SIP. The leadership team also shares and informs the rest of the staff about the content of the SIP and how the SIP is to be implemented. It is only through continuous analysis and monitoring of academic performance, demographic, process, and perception data can a self-sustaining school improvement be maintained.

NOTE

1. For more detail on the RCA process, please see chapter 2 in Frank S. Del Favero, ed., *Instructional Leadership: Knowledge and Skills for K–12 Success* (Lanham, MD: Rowman & Littlefield, 2019).

Chapter Three

Creating a Meaningful School Vision

Nancy P. Autin, PhD

A thriving, positive school culture is rooted in the minds and hearts of individuals who share common beliefs and a sense of purpose. Energy permeates the environment, communicating a shared commitment to individual and communal growth. This chapter emphasizes the role of creating and sustaining a meaningful school vision to ensure continuous school improvement. It highlights the importance of analyzing current data to identify strengths and opportunities for improvement.

SCHOOL VISION AND BELIEFS

When discussing a school governance's structure, its culture and climate, conversations inevitably involve reviewing the school's mission or vision statements. When visiting a school's website, parents, educators, and other visitors are likely to click on the school's mission or vision statement to get an immediate sense of what is important for that school. Some schools will have only one or the other, while others will have both a mission and a vision statement.

The life of a school or an organization begins with a group of individuals (or it may even be a single individual) contemplating these questions: Who are we? Why do we exist? What is our purpose? A succinctly written statement, the mission statement, answers these questions. Mission statements generally begin with or include these phrases: to offer, to provide, or to develop. In one or two compelling sentences, a mission statement tells what it does, for whom, and how it will do what it says it will do. Successful organizations define their identities, which leads to crafting a clear and meaningful vision for success.

While the emphasis here is on a school's establishment of a compelling vision statement, it is certainly worthwhile to see from the onset how mission and vision statements may differ for a school or organization. Let us consider the mission statements of three different levels of learning environments. In what way does each address one or more of the questions inherent in a mission statement: Who are we? Why do we exist? What is our purpose?

- The mission of B. Smart Elementary School is to develop well-rounded individuals who are lifelong learners and contributing citizens by providing a rigorous and caring environment that responds to the needs of the total child.
- The mission of Bright Minds High School is to partner with local businesses to help prepare students to develop the knowledge, skills, and work ethic to be responsible citizens and improve life in their local communities.
- "The B. I. Moody III College of Business Administration is a vibrant learning community in a culturally rich region. We foster intellectual curiosity, creativity, and innovation to produce a seasoned gumbo of successful professionals, scholars, and global citizens."[1]

Using these three examples, one can see there is no single universal phrase, statement, or group of statements that could ever represent the vision of diverse educational environments. It is a general principle that mission and vision are unique to an institution or school. The vision statement of each is deeply rooted in the values and beliefs embraced by a school community: administrators, faculty and staff, parents, students, and community. Using the present as the starting point, the vision points to a hope-filled future for its members. Revisiting our previous examples, the respective vision statements may well include a message similar to these:

- The vision at B. Smart Elementary School is to create a nationally known inner-city elementary school that produces major gains in student achievement and helps make the neighborhood in which it is located a better place to live and work.
- Bright Minds High School's vision is to create a secondary school that is highly regarded for its academic excellence, its leadership development, and its contribution in actively serving and improving the community in which it operates.
- "The vision of the B. I. Moody III College of Business Administration is to be recognized as a leader in developing ethically responsible professionals and scholars who positively impact our Acadiana region, Louisiana, and the global community."[2]

The direction and guidance to a successful future first depends on answering the question, What will our school look like in five years? That is, what will be different? Mission is about the present; vision looks to the future, what we will be in the years ahead. Because of this projection, a school's vision needs to be comprehensive. It may be a paragraph or several paragraphs. The vision statement paints a clear, inspiring, and compelling picture of the future if the mission of the school is carried out. The vision statement of Bright Minds High School describes how academic excellence will look in the future; it propels the school forward.

In order to determine what student learning and achievement will look like, to project a thriving learning environment for faculty and students, to connect school and community in meaningful ways, Bright Minds High School must begin with examining its current goals and practices, student academic performance, the learning environment, and the school's relationship with stakeholders and the community it serves. Before a new vision can be created, or an existing one modified, a process for carefully reviewing and analyzing current school documents and data is the critical first step.

ESTABLISHING A BASELINE: ANALYZING CURRENT SCHOOL DATA

Envisioning an inviting and invigorating future for a school is healthy for everyone; getting there is also the work of everyone. As conversations begin about where we want to be in the next five or ten years, school leaders realize the need to ponder the present before planning the future. It is akin to planning for a long trip with one's family. Family members ask questions such as, Where do we want to go? How long will it potentially take us to get there? What do we already have, and what additional information and resources do we need to ensure a successful journey? If we leave from our home, what route do we take to arrive at our desired destination?

The journey of creating a meaningful school vision begins with establishing a baseline: collecting and analyzing existing school data. It is the responsibility of school leaders to determine how this task will be accomplished. A team of individuals knowledgeable in collecting, analyzing, and interpreting data is the best way to ensure that this process has the greatest chance of being meaningful. This could also be an opportune time to invite new persons to the data collection and analysis process. By inviting them to join the team, they become a valuable resource in going forward in the decision-making process.

It is the responsibility of school leaders to provide the motivation, support, and clear directions to the team. Their task must be focused, and time must be provided for the team to do its work. While leaders should not micromanage the work of the data team, school leaders should monitor its ongoing progress and be available when help is needed. Most importantly, the team members must experience the trust and confidence that school leaders share with them in actively participating in establishing a basis for studying and planning the vision for the future of the school.

The school leader should be present at the first organizational meeting of the data team to communicate its important role in the initial—but—critical first phase of planning for a successful school future. The school leader will clearly describe the team's role in studying the school's current profile as revealed in school data. There can be no substitute for this work; that is, the school leader should not delegate this responsibility to someone else. Everyone should know that the school leader is at the helm. While the process is shared and owned by all, the leader of the school is the person who calls everyone to action.

DATA TEAM ORGANIZATION AND ACTIONS

The team is empowered to function collaboratively in completing the tasks entrusted to it. It is recommended that the team engage in these preliminary steps at its initial meeting:

- Select a facilitator from members of the team.
- Select a recorder for first meeting. (This task can be rotated.)
- Establish norms for working.
- Review goals of the team (provided by school leadership).
- Prioritize work (what needs to happen first and subsequently).
- Set meeting times, goals for next meeting, agenda items.

Prioritizing the work of the team from the onset will help the team function both effectively and efficiently. The team must identify what data are needed to provide a current profile of the school. Two major data categories are needed: student performance data and data pertaining to school climate and culture. Performance data include both standardized test results and teacher-made assessments. Performance data include teacher-student interactions in the learning and assessing process. Perception data capture stakeholders' opinions: governance, teaching and learning, the school environment, and community relationships and involvement.

To identify what data are needed, several key questions need to be answered. Since the work of the team will directly impact the future direction of the school, adopting a critical questions framework will guide the team. Some suggestions include the following:

- What performance data are available for review?
- What evidence are we looking for?
- Where and how are we going to find it?
- What gaps, if any, do we have in our understanding that will require more analysis to determine what is happening and why?
- What documentation will show this data to be valid and credible to all stakeholders?

In formulating responses to these questions, the team should do the following:

- Utilize a variety of data sources (from within the school and outside of school)
- Utilize multiple measures (school processes, student learning, demographics, perceptions)
- Study multiple levels of information and combinations of measures over time (e.g., math and science scores over three consecutive years)
- Use existing data as much as possible. Demographic and student learning data are typically available at the school or district level. However, it may be necessary to create tools to collect perceptual data.

As the team members analyze data and identify root causes, they will need to refine the questions they want to ask and identify pertinent data to be collected to answer these questions. When this happens, organizing subgroups within the team is recommended as an efficient way to proceed. Ultimately, this work will contribute to the school's vision for improvement, which will be captured in the articulation of well-defined school improvement goals and action steps to accomplish these goals.

IDENTIFYING STRENGTHS AND OPPORTUNITIES FOR IMPROVEMENT

An institution's ongoing success depends on collecting, analyzing, interpreting, and using existing data to guide the institution to the next level of success. Amanda Datnow, Vicki Park, and Priscilla Wohlstetter, in their work with the Center on Educational Governance at the University of Southern California, emphasize that data informs existing strengths and provides insight into areas needing attention while also guiding the improvement process systematically and strategically.[3] This is challenging intellectual work as it necessitates identifying gaps between a current state of student learning and school effectiveness and that which is desired.

Vision-based leadership understands the complexities of guiding a school from where it is today to a shared vision of future possibilities. Jerry D. Bamburg states, "Only when schools develop a shared understanding of current reality can a commitment to change be initiated and sustained."[4] School leaders and data teams must therefore first assist faculty in understanding where the school currently stands in order to discern where they want to go. Engaging faculty and staff in identifying the strengths and areas where growth is needed builds trust, supports participation in the process, and nurtures ownership in the school improvement process.

Vision-based leaders and their teams look to a variety of data to identify areas of strength and areas where improvement is needed. They look at the current vision or school goals to uncover places where goals have not been met. If goals were not previously set, then clearly shortcomings will emerge in these studies.

In addition to state, district, and local student achievement data, analyzing other data—including staff participation in professional learning opportunities, teacher turnover rates, grade-level planning, and parental and community involvement—will help the faculty gain the knowledge needed to identify areas of strength and areas in which to direct improvement efforts. Once this is done, faculty and stakeholders are ready to engage in meaningful conversations centered on developing a compelling vision statement.

BUILDING GOALS THROUGH STAKEHOLDER INVOLVEMENT

School leadership extends beyond the internal functioning of the school. Establishing and honoring positive relationships with stakeholders is a key factor in raising institutional quality. School leaders are responsible for ensuring that all learners achieve while also managing many other facets of an institution. Institutions that function effectively do so without tension between the administrators and educators and have established relationships of mutual respect emanating from a shared vision (Feuerstein & Opfer, 1998).

As reported in a meta-analysis of educational leadership research, Kenneth Leithwood and Jingping Sun found that leaders can significantly "influence school conditions through their achievement of a shared vision and agreed-on goals for the organization, their high expectations and support of organizational members, and their practices that strengthen school culture and foster collaboration within the organization."[5]

An effective school leader knows that the future of a school is not about individual goals; it is about the totality of the learning environment in the future. The overall task is complex; it takes into account one's personal beliefs and values in concert with those of the school and community. For this reason, the effective school leader uses team-building skills to draft an initial plan in collaboration with other school personnel to involve key stakeholders in the process of building goals. Including stakeholders in setting goals begins with answering several simple questions:

- Who must be involved?
- What forum will be used to bring stakeholders together?
- How will internal and external stakeholders collaborate?
- What steps and tools will be used to guide deliberations in formulating goals?

Initial Steps for Goal Setting

A facilitator is needed to guide this process. This person does not have to be the principal but must be someone who is well respected by school stakeholders.

1. Prepare tools to be used in the goal-setting process. Samples of these resources are available through educational organizations, accreditation agencies, and books by authors noted for their leadership in the school improvement process.
2. Form teams consisting of internal and external stakeholders (teachers, staff, parents, community members, and students). Each team will select a facilitator and a recorder.
3. Provide teams with the existing statement related to student learning, if one exists. What is still priority? What needs to change? Do this in conjunction with step 4. If no vision statement exists, move straight to step 4.
4. Provide teams with data summaries derived in the data analysis process (see section "Establishing a Baseline: Analyzing Current School Data"). The summaries will highlight both strengths and areas in need of improvement.
5. Ask each team to brainstorm the future desired outcome for student learning and school effectiveness based on data summaries.
6. Group like ideas into three main areas:

   - Student performance—knowledge, skills, and dispositions desired for all students
   - School effectiveness—organizational conditions/environment for maximal learning
   - School and community—relationship between school and community and impact that student learning has on the community

7. Craft a consensus statement incorporating each area of step 6. A single statement may incorporate desired learner outcomes together with a brief description of the future learning environment. The relationship between school and community may need to be a separate statement. There are multiple ways to approach goals. You may have one for each of the three areas in step 6. However, two concise and clearly written goals may be better, particularly in the area of needed improvement. Establishing one or two goals to bolster strengths are needed to maintain ongoing momentum. The action steps in this area are often easy to describe and should be included in the school improvement plan.

CRAFTING A REVISED OR NEW SCHOOL VISION

Revising an existing vision statement or writing a new one requires beginning with the end in mind. If a vision already exists, revisiting it in light of current data is imperative. This will provide evidence of how the institution is doing now. Reviewing current data provides evidence for what needs to happen moving forward. What changes have taken place in the school or community since the previous vision was crafted? What societal needs have changed? Questions such as these will play a major role in deciding what must be done. That is, can the existing vision be maintained? Or, should it be modified, or completely changed?

Crafting a desired future for learning is the cornerstone of the school improvement process. Borrowing from the National Study of School Evaluation (NSSE), two important steps must never be circumvented:

1. Study research practices aimed at improving student performance.
2. Articulate values and beliefs about student learning, future trends, and school-community relationships.[6]

These two steps are needed when reviewing an existing vision as well as in creating a new one.

Beginning with the end in mind necessitates asking what must be included in the final vision statement. Creating a rubric guided by NSSE's two principles will be helpful. Key elements are values and beliefs, best practices gleaned from research, and a future direction for expectations for learners and school effectiveness. These elements are described in the rubric, so the school community has a clearly defined backdrop of what is important in the vision.

- Research based: A comprehensive, articulate, research-supported statement describes the school's focus, the intended learning culture, and the characteristics that would distinguish this school from another. The vision statement articulates moving a school beyond its current state.
- Direction and expectations: The vision clearly allows the reader to see what students will look like when they complete the school's program of studies. It includes what they will know and be able to do. It is relevant to individual, community, and societal needs. It speaks to students and their roles as members of a community and the impact that they will have.
- Beliefs: The vision statement provides a clear, comprehensive articulation of nonnegotiable leadership and stakeholder beliefs. Beliefs are aligned with student learning and expectations of graduates as envisioned. Leadership is shared and collegial rather than authoritative. The focus is on promoting positive student achievement and growth.

CHAPTER SUMMARY

A meaningful school vision is based on an examination of the current status of the school and involves an analysis of data. These data consist of four distinct types of data: academic, demographic, process, and perceptions. A careful interpretation of the data will represent the current status of the school. One may find areas of concern in academic data, such as scores in a specific subject area or grade level. School process data that includes information regarding student discipline, for example, may indicate problems in the area of classroom management.

Once areas of concern that characterize the current status of the school have been identified, members of the vision team can begin the vision-building process. The ultimate goal of the vision team is to create a vision that defines the characteristics that school stakeholders want to see the school acquire.

The school vision is based on outcomes. The vision captures what graduates of the school will look like when they leave the school. It is developed collaboratively and reflects the values and beliefs of school leaders and all stakeholders. It is original and inspiring. It is well grounded in current research promoting high expectations and strategies for achieving desired results. The defining characteristics of the vision must be evident in the overall school improvement plan as discussed in chapter 2.

NOTES

1. "Our Mission," University of Louisiana at Lafayette B. I. Moody III College of Business Administration, https://business.louisiana.edu/about-us/our-mission.

2. "Our Mission."

3. Amanda Datnow, Vicki Park, and Priscilla Wohlstetter, *Achieving with Data: How High-Performing School Systems Use Data to Improve Instruction for Elementary Students* (Los Angeles: Center on Educational Governance, University of Southern California, 2007).

4. Jerry D. Bamburg, *Raising Expectations to Improve Student Learning*, Urban Monograph Series (Oak Brook, IL: North Central Regional Educational Lab, 1994), 23.

5. Kenneth Leithwood and Jingping Sun, "The Nature and Effects of Transformational School Leadership: A Meta-analytic Review of Unpublished Research," *Educational Administration Quarterly* 48 no. 387 (2012): 388–423.

6. National Study of School Evaluation, *Breakthrough School Improvement: An Action Guide for Greater and Faster Results*, July 2005.

Chapter Four

Community Engagement

Tarrah C. Davis, EdD

Educational leaders foster community engagement by bridging the school and community together via effective communication. This chapter will help create an awareness and value of public relations and community engagement that in turn will impact an improved school culture that nurtures student achievement. Effective community engagement does not just happen on its own, but requires an understanding of the school and community, goals, current usable data, connections, and using effective forms of communication.

It is important for educational leaders to understand the importance of stakeholder perceptions of the school and its community. The school is an integral part of the community, and establishing and nurturing connections with parents and the community is essential for success. There are different types of school and community relations communication plans. These plans must be well thought out, initiated, analyzed, and reviewed continuously. Current effective use of technologies used by the parents, school, stakeholders, and community should be established in order to improve school and community communications.

SCHOOL AND COMMUNITY RELATIONS COMMUNICATION PLANS

An effective communication plan follows the mission, vision, and goals for the school or school district. It takes into account the school demographics and community, identifies needs, and is constantly monitored and evaluated. A communication plans uses data collected from a comprehensive analysis from a school or school district, and it provides interventions and/or activities to address the data analysis.

A school and community relations communication plan creates a foundation to help link the school and community together. It is built upon research. It requires finding out who you are as a community and a school, understanding and working closely with your stakeholders, and keeping the lines of communication open and free from misunderstandings. The list below shows components that may be included in a school and community relations communication plan:

- Mission, vision, goals, purpose
- Contextual design (school demographics and community)
- Stakeholders
- Needs assessment
- Activities and strategies
- Timeline
- Monitoring
- Evaluation

MISSION, VISION, GOALS, PURPOSE

As an educational leader, one must first identify and review the mission, vision, goals, and purpose of your school and district. If these are currently out of date and use, the revision or update may be one's first line of business. Just as teachers rely on standards and goals to create lesson plans, activities, and assessments to ensure that students are successful, a school and district must be aware of, understand, and follow the mission, vision, goals, and purpose. Otherwise, the ultimate goals are already unreachable.

The communication plan must begin with these things in mind. As the communication plan is in place, it is important to circle back to make sure that the plan is helping to meet the mission, vision, goals, and purpose of the school and community.[1]

CONTEXTUAL DESIGN (SCHOOL DEMOGRAPHICS AND COMMUNITY)

What is known about the school and community? One must gather important information regarding the following:

- The school's performance rating and its improvement plan
- Demographic data and information regarding the area in which the school is located

- Funding allocations for the school
- Current educational policies for the school, the district, and the state
- The extent that these policies are aligned with state and federal laws
- The extent that technology and social media are used in the school and district.

The contextual design of the communication plan includes all the information above. It helps create a picture of the school and community. Creating a contextual design of the school not only helps to make educational leaders aware, but it helps teachers, parents, stakeholders, and the community have a better understanding of the status and functions of the school itself.

STAKEHOLDERS

Effective communication plans require effective communication and a process that involves not just parents and teachers, but other stakeholders in the community as well. When stakeholders are involved with gathering information, decision-making, and problem solving, they have a better understanding of why decisions were made. Many times, they also bring in resources otherwise not provided to the school system.

Educating children takes a village. Stakeholders are a vital part of the village. An effective school and community relations communication plan requires the creation of a committee. This committee should include key stakeholders such as students, parents, teachers, administrators, and community members.

NEEDS ASSESSMENT

A needs assessment permits schools the opportunity to assess their existing communication approach and policies. It tells educational leaders and stakeholders what the "needs" are for the schools. The needs assessment is designed to "measure attitudes and opinions of internal and external publics, and to determine what should be done to increase public understanding, support, and participation in the district."[2] This needs assessment may be designed by a committee, or it may be a questionnaire/survey available to the school.

A needs assessment should include at least three basic sections. The introduction section should contain the purpose and a brief explanation. The main section of the needs assessment should consist of opinion questions that pertain to what the school is attempting to gain information about. The conclusion of this questionnaire should include open-ended questions so that the stakeholders have an opportunity to share information that may not be requested but is important to the respondent. The needs assessment gives schools the opportunity to get feedback from a multitude of stakeholders without using a lot of manpower or money. This feedback provides excellent data and may give information on valuable unused resources.

Data collected and analyzed from the needs assessment should be examined through the lens of vision, mission, and goals and should answer the question, How does the information gathered compare to the actual vision and mission of the school? The answers to this question will aid in the development and creation of a communication plan that includes (a) refining vision and mission statements and (b) establishing communication plan goals and objectives. Once the plan is established, the first order is to decide which issue(s) to target.

ACTIVITIES AND STRATEGIES

Once a needs assessment is completed, activities and strategies need include setting goals. These goals are the anticipated results of the communication plan, which should be specific, measurable, attainable, relevant, and timely. Educational leaders should map these out on a timeline as shown below. Technology used by the students, public, and stakeholders should be considered when choosing activities, strategies, and committee members. It is vital that communication plans incorporate changing technologies used by all involved.

Being proactive is much better than being reactive when communicating and preparing. It is an excellent idea to incorporate ways to communicate with students, parents, faculty, and stakeholders for many different scenarios, emergencies, or crises. For example, for an educational leader, what are some emergencies that may require immediate communication?

- Bad weather (tornadoes, flooding, hurricane, etc.)
- School lockdown
- Bomb threat
- Emergency vehicles in front of school
- Fire or fire drill
- Death of a student or faculty member

A good idea would be to brainstorm with other leaders of different types of emergencies that may occur or may have occurred in other schools and districts to get a more comprehensive list. (One must also not forget to make local law enforcement and emergency personnel a part of the school's crisis management team.) The crisis management team can use the list of potential emergencies to develop appropriate forms of communication and content that address a variety of emergency situations.

By being proactive and developing a series of responses for each potential emergency situations, the crisis management team, during the time of an actual crisis, can initiate a predeveloped and tailored response and be able devote itself more directly to the situation at hand. One must keep in mind the need to regularly review and revise over time the predeveloped responses.

For example, an electronic phone call to home numbers may be the most effective form of communication during the current year; however, one may discover that fewer and fewer parents answer their phones. A more effective way to "call out" to parents may be text messages. A revised method of communication during an emergency could include a combination of a call-out, an email, and/or information posted on social media outlets.

As responsibilities of an administrator, these email groups, callout messages, or whichever form of communication is chosen can be saved and prepared well ahead of an emergency. Access can be given to specific staff or administrative positions so that several different people are ready if an emergency were to occur. These communication measures will also need to be considered as progress is made throughout the entire communication plan as goals are being worked on and met.

TIMELINE

A communication plan timeline should consist of several basic sections including the goals, activities, performance measures, person(s) responsible, and target completion date. It may also include time frame, resources needed, cost/fund account, frequency of meetings (weekly/monthly), and so forth. The timeline below is a sample of how you can plan overall goals and objectives. Some goals/objectives and activities may have to be further broken down into checklists in order to make them more manageable.

MONITORING

In order for a communication plan to be effective, it must be monitored and tasks must be followed throughout. Monitoring should occur on a regular basis for each goal, for each activity, and with those responsible. Throughout this process, unforeseen things will occur and changes and modifications will need to be made based on the needs of the students, school, and community.

Items may need to be added or taken away, order of priority may change, and dates may change. The monitoring process is extremely important because without it, things may fall to the wayside. Plan the monitoring process.

Table 4.1. Sample Timeline

Goals/ Objectives	Activities	Performance Measures	Person(s) Responsible	Target Date

How will an educational leader monitor the progress of each objective? How will he or she communicate the results? What are some effective forms of communication for each objective or person(s) responsible (e.g., GroupMe, Remind, text, email, weekly meetings)?

EVALUATION

Part of a good communication plan involves measuring results. Have the objectives of the plan been met? What worked; what didn't work? Are there newly identified needs or concerns? Evaluation of the plan can be done in various ways including monthly, annually, and after major milestones in the preestablished timelines. Examples of ways to communicate progress may be through monthly or bimonthly reports on the work in progress, official committee reports, and/or annual summary reports. The evaluation should be included within the timeline and scheduled accordingly.

SCHOOL AND COMMUNITY PARTNERSHIP

There are many reasons the school and community should work as a partnership. Developing this partnership can improve how the students succeed at school as well as later in life and in their communities. The school should be an essential part of the community. A community and school partnership can "improve school programs and school climate, provide family services and support, increase parents' skills and leadership, connect families with others in the school and in the community, and help teachers with their work."[3]

One should not fail to search for and learn from examples of strong and effective school and community partnerships. Successful partnerships can be found within the school district or in neighboring districts. An examination of current school and community partnerships may reveal relationships that can be strengthened and expanded. The findings of the needs assessment can form the basis of change. Once the community begins to see the school's willingness and intent to develop and refine school and community partnerships, community stakeholders will begin to develop an interest and they will begin to feel vested in the school.

What are the best ways for a school to communicate effectively with the community and keep it engaged? Does the local TV station or newspaper regularly report on and highlight activities of students and teachers? How active are local stakeholders on social media? Could the local social media be used to inform the public about students and school activities?

A productive partnership includes interactions that flow both ways: school to community and community to school. A great deal of untapped potential resources may be discovered in the community by simply providing forums that allow discussions on a variety of school/community topics. This may begin with a survey of the community, school, and stakeholders to find out more but then must result in a plan of action and follow-up.

CONNECTIONS WITH PARENTS

Connections with parents must be proactive and ongoing. They should not begin with an impersonal list of school discipline rules and end with report cards. Meaningful and effective school-to-home communications entail much more. Parents should be aware of the mission, vision, and goals of the school. They need to know that their perceptions and those of their children are important and that parental input is encouraged and appreciated.

When parents know what is expected of their children, they are more willing to support the schools. Similarly, as with connections to the community, parents need more detailed and frequent communications with the school. The methods and content of communication may vary depending on the educational and economic characteristics of the population. Communications will also vary based on the source of the communication, such as from school administrators to parents or from teachers to parents.

It is important to know the characteristics of the audience targeted by the communication. This will help to determine the more appropriate modes of communication, such as email, texting, regular mail, or social media. One needs to be aware that a variety of modes of communication may be necessary to get out a message.

Unfortunately, in many instances, communications between the school and the home tend to be negative in nature. These negative communications address poor grades, discipline infractions on the part of the student, or requests for money to cover fines and/or fees. In short, most parents perceive school-to-home communications in a negative light. An effective communication plan will focus on changing parental perceptions of communications from school from negative to positive.

THE ROLE OF TEACHERS

School leaders should encourage, if not require, teachers to make contact with parents at the start of every school year for the purpose of introducing themselves to them and to say something kind about their child. Having teachers start the year with a positive communication will do a great deal to improve the nature of school-to-home communications.

Some examples of positive school-to-home communications include, but are not limited to, the following:

- Welcoming parents to open houses
- Announcing events and opportunities for them to volunteer at them
- Having teachers send postcards to parents each month with a positive note regarding their child
- Creating a school newsletter (the old-fashioned paper kind and/or electronically) that highlights educational programs, student achievements, and accomplishments by various members of the teaching staff

One should remember that communication is bidirectional. Offer information to parents, but also find avenues to receive information from parents. Unfortunately, in many schools, parents usually only receive information when something negative is happening. On the other hand, schools/teachers only hear from parents to report or comment on negative events or issues. An effective communication plan provides parents opportunities to communicate the positive things going on in school.

COMMUNITY BUSINESS CONNECTIONS

Students in today's classrooms will become members of tomorrow's society. Nurturing the connection between the school and the community businesses is vital for developing successful citizens of the future. The business community can provide resources and leadership, as well as serve as role models for students. Cultivating these connections provides opportunities for students to see and experience what is possible.

An examination of the needs assessment data may identify possible links and connections with local businesses that may benefit the school. Such a connection may help to develop an association with a food and beverage supplier. This could result in free or reduced costs to cover concessions sold at local sporting events. Associations with local department stores and sporting goods retailers could be a source of prizes and awards for school events. The possibilities are endless when the school and business connections are cultivated.

SCHOOL AND COMMUNITY (STAKEHOLDER PERCEPTIONS)

The connections among the school, parents, business leaders, and other community stakeholders are important and should be encouraged and nurtured. Stakeholders may be local elected leaders, administrators, parents, families, school faculty and staff, school board members, district leaders, and state and national leaders. In short, stakeholders are community members who are vested in the overall success of the students, the school, and the community. Vested stakeholders recognize the fact that the school and the community are interdependent where the success of the community impacts the success of the school and vice versa.

In order to foster an atmosphere of interdependence, we must understand the current perceptions of school and community stakeholders. In order to do this, perception data must be gathered. This is usually done through survey questions on a needs assessment, interviews, or focus groups. An analysis of the perception data will reveal negative perceptions held by stakeholders. Efforts would then address interventions and strategies designed to change negative perceptions.

CHAPTER SUMMARY

Effective community engagement consistently fostered by educational leaders can help bridge the gap between the school and community. In order for this to occur, a continuous understanding of the goals of the school and community, perceptions, connections, communications, and carefully thought-out plans should be reviewed continuously. Communication plans can guide this process beginning with the mission, vision, and goals. These plans identify needs and initiate the creation of a foundation to link the school and community.

This chapter highlights the components that should be included in an effective school and community relations communication plan. It includes valuable information regarding needs assessment, activities and strategies, ways to be proactive, creating timelines, and the importance of monitoring and evaluating the plan.

Building partnerships between the school and community while establishing and nurturing connections with parents and community businesses all help to build community engagement. The importance of understanding the stakeholder perceptions of the school and its community and the building of this understanding is also vital for effective community engagement. Community engagement and communication plans are not one-time events but rather should be consistently revisited and revised to foster continuous, effective engagement and improvement.

NOTES

1. Julia Ballenger, "How to Develop a Communications/School-Community Relations Plan," *International Journal of Educational Leadership Preparation* 5, no. 3 (2010): 1–7.

2. D. R. Gallagher, D. Bagin, and E. H. Moore, *The School and Community Relations*, 8th ed. (Boston: Pearson/Allyn and Bacon, 2005), 26.

3. Joyce L. Epstein, *School, Family, and Community Partnerships: Preparing Educators and Improving Schools* (Boulder, CO: Westview, 2010), 389.

Chapter Five

Inspiring and Leading the Change Process

Erin Stokes, EdD

A new principal hosts the first faculty meeting of the year. He delivers an inspiring message about the urgent need for student growth and data-driven decisions. The focus then becomes the teacher handbook, which includes discipline policies, dress code guidelines, and an overview of substitute requests. The teachers sign that they have received the handbook and are sent to begin lesson planning before the students arrive the next day.

Unfortunately, two months later, the principal finds that the same teachers who seemed enthusiastic about the year are not turning in lesson plans on time, they are late to team meetings, and they complain about student issues outside of their realm of influence. Trying to initiate change seems almost impossible. The school has quickly become the way it used to be—a cesspool of negativity and apathy.

THE CHIEF CHANGE AGENT

Quite often new principals inherit issues from the previous faculty and administration. This is one reason why understanding the change process is so important. In order to reach the highest levels of achievement, teachers and administrators must embrace change.

Principals are the chief change agents. Most often, change begins with the leader and is executed by the teachers. Just as the Olympic torch is carried from city to city around the world, the principal is the torch lighter and the teachers carry the flame.

For the most part, people readily embrace medical advances. If a person today were scheduled to undergo a delicate spinal surgery, most likely he or she would opt to use a doctor with current knowledge and technology. Who would want to use medical practices from twenty years ago? Interestingly, doctors build upon previous knowledge to inform new advances in the medical field.

Unfortunately, educators often do not always readily accept change. Perhaps this is because change rarely lasts in a school system. Unlike medical researchers who continue to use long-standing practices that are successful while incorporating current practices, educational leaders tend to have knee-jerk reactions and launch brand-new initiatives before seeing the progress from the previous fad. Changes that do not become part of the culture of an organization do not last, and stakeholders see change as another interruption in the system.

Although imbedding changes into the culture of a school is not always easy, this chapter addresses school culture and gives leaders practical ways to introduce change, implement it, and sustain it.

CHAPTER PREVIEW

This chapter is organized into five major sections: understanding change, readiness for change, initiating the change, change implementation, and sustainability. Readers will gain an understanding of each stage of the change process as well as practical ideas that school leaders can easily implement.

UNDERSTANDING CHANGE

Robert Marzano's descriptions of the two types of change are widely used in education circles.[1] First-order change describes incremental changes that are relatively easy to implement. This type of change relies on previous patterns and thinking that have been successful. For instance, changing the duty schedules of teachers in order to pair planning partners together would be a first-order change. A change in the bell schedule to accommodate a new reading program would be a first-order change. These changes often affect the climate of the school.

Second-order changes are much more drastic and, therefore, problematic. However, this does not mean one should avoid second-order changes. These changes are what makes organizations grow. Unlike first-order change, second-order change requires new ways of thinking. Problems are solved by using innovative philosophies. An example of a second-order change would be math and science teachers planning year-round project-based units together for seventh and eighth graders.

In order for second-order changes to be sustained, they must be embedded in the culture of the school. Without the needed supports and strong leadership in place, the second-order change will fail, and things will go back to the way they were. The change must become *the way we do things here* and *part of who we are*. It should be every leader's goal to make successful changes in a school that become part of the school's identity.

However, creating second-order change that becomes the way of life for a school faculty is not easy. There is a process by which change unfolds. There are three stages of change: initiation, implementation, and sustainability.[2] *Initiation* of change is the point at which the idea is born and discussed among organizational leaders. The vision is created and the action plan is drafted. Stakeholders are invited to share in the planning process, and all members of the organization are made aware of the upcoming change. One can imagine drafting the blueprints and pouring the foundation for a house. These critical parts of the process of building a house can affect the strength of the building for its entire existence.

Implementation is the point at which the change is enacted. Much support and problem solving is required during this stage. The vision as well as the action plan must be clear. Lack of clarity is detrimental to the change process. Leaders should be continually taking the pulse of the organization, which includes assessing the change process, replenishing needed resources, and providing ongoing professional development to teachers.

Sustainability is the point at which the change becomes part of the school's culture. The organization has infused the change as part of its typical work, and the members of the organization work to sustain the change. A leader's work is not over during this stage. Sustainability requires continued attention and subtle shifts to make the change last. Like most organizations, school demographics and stakeholder needs change. Teachers have embraced the change as the norm in their school, and they work with the leaders to adjust the reform to fit the needs of the organization. Sustainability also includes working toward short-term goals and celebrating when success is achieved.

The remainder of the chapter will further discuss each stage of change in more detail. However, before implementing any second-order change, leaders should determine if the organization is ready for such change. If not, each stage of change will suffer and sustainability will not occur.

READINESS FOR CHANGE

Some schools endure change successfully, and others do not. One may imagine a science experiment with two beakers present. The first beaker represents a school with a strong culture and a positive climate. Teachers work together to solve problems, and leadership is shared. The other beaker represents a toxic school culture. Negativity toward students, teachers, and the leaders is a common practice. Teachers feel that they have no effect on student achievement, and the factors outside the school are too much to overcome.

The same reform is then placed in both beakers. Although the reform disrupts the first beaker, as all reforms do, eventually the reform dissolves into the liquid. It becomes part of the school's culture. Although the scientist knows that the reform is there, the liquid looks as it did previously. However, in the second beaker, the reform causes an explosion, breaking the glass and spilling out the liquid. The same reform placed in a different setting can have damaging effects on a school. Money is wasted, teachers leave the school and the profession, and time is lost.

Millions of dollars have been poured into low-performing schools, only for those schools to continue the pattern of decline. From a district or state perspective, the sense of urgency to change low-performing schools is compelling. Furthermore, low-performing schools tend to have more money available in the form of Title funds.

CASE STUDY

A district receives a grant to implement a new teacher improvement system that has a proven track record of being wildly successful. The teacher improvement system includes a new teacher evaluation tool, coaching and mentoring protocols, an online bank of resources, and a new system for professional learning community (PLC) meetings. The district leaders choose three of the lowest-performing schools in the district to participate. All three of the schools have been graded an F by the state letter grade accountability system. The schools receive additional personnel to assist the teachers by focusing on classroom practices. Systems are put in place to initiate and implement the reform, and district personnel are hired to oversee the change.

Two years later, the district superintendent makes a proposal to the school board members to close one of the schools and merge the other two schools in hopes that the drastic changes in administrators and personnel will provide a clean slate to begin again. The teacher improvement system that has the extremely high success rate did not improve anything. In fact, one of the schools dropped even more in its student performance scores.

READINESS FOR REFORM MATTERS

There are five key elements that have a strong relationship with reform: school culture, school climate, teacher efficacy, collective efficacy, and change leadership. What is even more powerful about these elements is that they also impact student achievement. The schools in the case study example struggled because their cultures were toxic. The leaders were new, and some considered them ineffective. Additionally, these leaders inherited or hired ineffective teachers. The level of collective efficacy at all three schools was very low.

SCHOOL CULTURE VERSUS SCHOOL CLIMATE

School leaders and teachers often refer to school culture and school climate as if they are the same. Although they are similar, leaders need to understand each construct individually. School culture is the foundation for school climate. Douglas Fiore presents the visual metaphor of an iceberg to describe the difference between culture and climate as well as the connection between the two:

> To understand the subtle differences between culture and climate, one must visualize a giant iceberg floating in the Northern Atlantic. The mass of ice that one is able to see in the frigid water represents school climate, in that it is readily observable. Just as one can easily perceive qualities and characteristics of the iceberg, the same qualities and characteristics are easily observable within the climate in a school. However, it is common knowledge that there is much more to the block of ice floating in the water. In fact, there is a giant mass of ice below the surface that is not visible or observable to the eye. This mass below the surface is not only larger, but more complex, and therefore provides the supporting structures necessary for the existence of the part that one is able to actually see. This large foundation that is not visible represents culture within the school; thus it is the supporting structure on which the climate rests. The shape of it undergoes a slower, but more purposeful change than does the more easily observable climate. Likewise, with the iceberg, the mass below the surface is stable and very difficult to modify; however, its counterpart above sea level is victim to many environmental factors which cause more rapid changes such as sun, wind, and rain.[3]

School climate is the general feeling or atmosphere in the school. It is the character of the school and the attitudes behind that character. School climate can change very easily—sometimes on a week-to-week basis depending on outside influences. School climate researchers tend to focus on organizational members' perceptions about the school environment. Culture researchers ask questions concerning members' beliefs about themselves.

School culture is rooted in deep-seated beliefs and operational frameworks. School culture is revealed in the values of the organizational members and the purpose behind their work. The traditions and stories that are passed down from teacher to teacher over generations become part of the culture as well. Tacit assumptions are most influential on school culture.[4] Examples of these said assumptions are premises about trust, relationships, loyalty, values, knowledge, and truth. These assumptions affect an organization in numerous ways, including how people approach problems and how motivated they are to change. There are major effects that school culture has on the organization.

School culture:

- Shapes behavior
- Builds community and commitment
- Increases motivation
- Improves school effectiveness and student achievement.[5]

Although school culture research is extensive, the following overarching themes and indicators of a strong culture exist: a focus on learning, collaboration, goal setting, and a sense of community. While leadership is not listed, it is the essential element that drives the previously mentioned themes of school culture.

CASE STUDY

A principal calls the faculty together to discuss the new teacher evaluation system that will be implemented in the current year by the state. He explains that teachers will be evaluated using a new rubric and by using students' growth on the state standardized test scores using a value-added model. This is not exciting news for the teachers—they are worried about how they will rank among their peers and about their unmotivated students. In the weeks that follow, the teachers become more tense among themselves and more intense with their students.

The principal calls a faculty meeting and pointedly addresses the concerns and the behaviors of the teachers. He encourages them to do what they normally do—work together to overcome the situation. The teachers listen and do what was suggested by their leader. They begin meeting after school and studying the new rubric. They look at data during PLCs. Quickly the climate of the school returns to the positive feeling it once had. The culture of the school becomes more powerful than the negative climate that was present for those few weeks. Culture influences climate.

TEACHER EFFICACY

Self-efficacy refers to one's sense of belief in himself that he will accomplish a specific task with competence. Self-efficacy is much different than self-esteem or self-concept, which refer to the person's whole self-image. Self-efficacy focuses on a specific domain. A person may have high efficacious beliefs concerning his basketball skills while having low efficacious beliefs in his ability to play an instrument. Teacher efficacy, therefore, refers to a teacher's belief that he can teach all students and help them learn.

Leaders must consider the efficacious beliefs of teachers because they affect several things, namely, student achievement. Efficacious teachers are better at student questioning, have a stronger focus on student learning, have stronger classroom management techniques, are willing to try new classroom strategies, and are more willing to change practices. When faced with a new curriculum or teaching strategy, these teachers tend to embrace the challenge instead of grumbling and complaining about it.

If teacher efficacy has such substantial impacts, leaders must be aware of the path to increasing efficacious beliefs. Albert Bandura outlined the four sources of efficacy in his early work: mastery experiences, vicarious experiences, verbal persuasion, and physiological factors. These same sources are considered valid today.[6]

Mastery experiences are the personal experiences one has with success at a specific task. When a teacher incorporates a new discussion strategy that is successful, she experiences an increase in efficacy. Vicarious experiences occur when a teacher sees another teacher of similar ability accomplish a task with success.

Verbal persuasion is hearing others confirm that the person can indeed experience success with the task. People have the easiest access to verbal persuasion, although the influence of said persuasion depends on the reliability of the source.

Collective efficacy is the new hot topic among educators. In his meta-analyses, John Hattie found that collective efficacy was more powerful than all the constructs he studied—even more powerful than socioeconomic status, response to intervention, and classroom management.[7] Unlike many may assume, collective efficacy is not the compounding of individuals' efficacious beliefs. Collective efficacy is a *group attribute* that takes on new significance for the organization.

For instance, a new teacher may have low efficacious beliefs for herself, but when she assesses the abilities of the entire faculty, she believes that together they can make a positive impact on student achievement. The opposite is true as well. A highly effective teacher with strong efficacious beliefs about himself may not believe that the whole faculty can positively impact students.

Collective efficacy is especially vital and influential for school-wide changes. The way the whole group believes about themselves is highly influential on the achievements of the group. School faculties that have strong efficacious beliefs accomplish more together. Although each teacher is a change agent and impacts his or her classroom, school-wide changes are accomplished by the entire group. A staff can be influenced by pressure to raise test scores, behavioral issues with students, policy changes, and the lack of parental involvement. Leaders must be mindful of these influences on collective efficacy, which trickle down to each individual classroom and student.

When planning a new initiative or a school-wide change, leaders should assess the health of the organization by considering school culture and climate, teacher efficacy, and collective efficacy. Just as the first case study described, if these constructs are not strengthened, the school-wide change will not be as successful.

One way to assess the organizational readiness for change is by using the Reform Readiness Survey, which measures the strength of school culture and climate in relation to change, teacher efficacy in relation to change, collective efficacy in relation to change, and change leadership.[8]

INITIATING THE CHANGE

After determining the organization's readiness for change, the leader is ready to embark on the change process. The first stage of the change process is initiation. As mentioned earlier, the initiation stage sets the foundation and the framework on which the change can be built. Readiness for reform is having the solid ground on which to build in the first place!

When people hear about a change, their first reaction is to think of how the change will personally affect them. Then, they want to understand why the change is needed. If the proposed change is not founded in a moral purpose—why we do what we do—then the teachers will not fully invest in the change.[9] People are driven by purpose, and if faculty members do not understand why the change is important for students or the greater society, they are more likely to resist the change. Also, leaders must evaluate whether the proposed change is necessary by asking these questions: How will it impact students? Is the change needed? Why is it needed?

Leaders must also communicate their vision for the change. However, the faculty is more likely to acquire that same vision if members are involved in the process of creating the vision. Furthermore, the vision for the change must align to the vision and mission of the school. If the two do not align, the school vision or the vision for the change needs to be amended. If the proposed change does not match the vision of the school, most likely the change is not founded in the school's moral purpose.

Ideally, the leader and the faculty leadership team will work together to form the vision for the change. Teachers want to know what the change process will look like and what it will be like when the change is fully in place. Transparency and clarity are better than shrouded plans.

Vision must be accompanied by the action plan. Again, the leadership team, or the entire faculty, should be involved in the creation of an action plan. They are more likely to take ownership of the plan and see that it is successful if they have a part in the creation of the plan. Each step must be detailed and easy to follow. Confusion breeds resistance to the change.

Involving teachers in the decision-making process will ensure success. New principals should almost immediately find the leaders among the faculty who exhibit best practices and are influential on other teachers. Finding teachers who represent different grade levels and/or subject areas will ensure that the special interests of teachers are addressed. Teachers are incredibly valuable in the change process. Utilizing them will strengthen their own leadership abilities as well.

It may be difficult for a new leader to find the teacher leaders in an unfamiliar faculty. One simple way to determine who to recruit to the leadership team is to ask. New principals can likely ask the previous principal or central office personnel to direct them to at least one influential, trustworthy teacher on the faculty. That teacher can then recruit others to the leadership team or convey the names of other leaders among the faculty to the principal. However, one must be careful to show equal favor to all teachers, whether or not they are on the leadership team. Furthermore, leaders must be aware of the possibility of cliques forming. Allowing cliques to form can quickly create a toxic work environment.

The leadership team and members of the faculty can be helpful in determining possible problems before they exist. Some leaders will sit with their leadership team and list possible complications and solutions. Sometimes the problems are easily solved before they happen. Conversations such as this should continue throughout the change process. The more problems that occur throughout the process, the more opportunities there are for teachers and students to be critical of the change itself. Minimizing disruptions during the normal workings of the school will create a natural environment for both the teachers and the students—even during a major change.

The principal is most often the chief communicator with the central office. Sometimes the change may originate from district personnel. In these cases, the district usually provides the resources needed for students and teachers. However, if the principal initiates the change, he or she needs the support from district personnel in several ways.

First, leaders must seek permission to embark on certain changes, depending on how the change may affect instructional minutes, resource distribution, or the community. Having the support from the district superintendent makes the change process much easier for the principal. Second, many districts dictate how funds are spent on textbooks and supplies. Funds can be allocated to support the change within the school, and often the district gives further support in the form of resources if it is supportive of the change.

Third, the district may offer support in the form of personnel. Curriculum specialists or instructional coaches may be instrumental in supporting the change.

Lastly, the community can be instrumental in supporting the change or making it much harder. Not all changes will require leaders to conjure community support; however, second-order changes that affect the whole school are almost guaranteed to have community input, whether or not one asks for it. Some ways to amass support is to invite community leaders and parents to communicate the proposed changes to them. Again, it is imperative to begin with moral purpose, answering the questions, Why do we need this change? How will this affect my child? They need the opportunity to ask questions and discuss concerns. Giving the community opportunities to support the school in the change process will prove valuable in sustaining the efforts of the reform.

In summary, it is critical to share in the decision-making process concerning the vision and the action plan. All steps must be communicated clearly to the teachers. Resources must be available and proper professional development must occur *before* the change is implemented. Teachers will be frustrated with a lack of resources and anxious without the proper training to implement the reform. Attacking problems before they occur will minimize false starts and interruptions during instructional time. Involving the district personnel and community members will only strengthen the reform.

IMPLEMENTATION CASE STUDY

The day finally came to implement the recently planned Response to Intervention block for all sixth, seventh, and eighth graders at a failing school. The time block was created to meet students' needs in reading and math on their individual levels across the school. Students were grouped according to their standardized test scores.

Teachers had their new rosters. They had instructions to have students complete a pretest during the first week of intervention. Students were called to the auditorium and new schedules were given. During the first few days, there were several confused sixth graders who did not know what class to attend, but for the most part the teachers and the students found their new rhythm in the reform.

Unfortunately, this was just the beginning of the coming chaos. Some of the teachers were still waiting on resources. Others needed help understanding how to use the resources. Students' schedules still needed to be tweaked so they could attend the appropriate class for their reading levels. After the pretest was finished, the teachers scrambled to find resources. Little was communicated to the teachers on how to address the students' needs at each level.

The principal pushed to have the reform start before all the pieces were put into place, and because of this, each day the teachers grew more and more frustrated. Some of the teachers completely stopped teaching during the block. What was supposed to be additional help for struggling students quickly became a waste of time.

As previously mentioned, the initiation stage of the change process can make the implementation a success, or it can cause it to fall apart, just like the blueprints and the foundation of a home are vital to the sturdiness of the building. Implementing reform hastily will almost certainly result in failure. Sometimes slower is better.

If the reform is well planned, the initiation will be almost seamless. However, leaders cannot foresee every problem. Each organization is very different and complex. When implementing a second-order change, the leader must be visible and available during the implementation. Leaders cannot troubleshoot problems or guide the reform if they are not present during the implementation. Second-order reform cannot be an afterthought or completely delegated to other leaders. Although delegation of responsibilities is helpful and necessary, the leader is the visionary, guiding the change process.

Teachers need to know that the leader is in control, and they want to trust that the leader will communicate any issues or minor changes to the action plan. They like to be consulted throughout the process and made aware of what they are doing correctly. Teachers value being valued!

A teacher once stated, "I'd rather have the resources that I need for my classroom than the promise of a bonus for good test scores. I end up buying almost everything I need anyway." This frustrated teacher taught at a turnaround school in which resources were not properly allocated by the principal. Reform does not work if the resources are not supplied and replenished. Leaders sometimes forget to allocate the resources for the future. Purchasing 150 laptops at one time may not be as wise as purchasing 100 laptops and parts for the maintenance of the technology-enhanced whiteboards in the classrooms. Sustainability is the goal.

Since teacher efficacy and collective efficacy influence both reform and student achievement, it is imperative that leaders keep a pulse on their teachers' behaviors associated with their beliefs. Both teacher efficacy and collective efficacy, although very different constructs, can be increased on an individual level and collectively by using the four sources of efficacy: mastery experiences, vicarious experiences, verbal persuasion, and physiological factors.

Practically speaking, each teacher needs to experience success with the reform. This is mastery experience. But in order to experience success, the principal must equip teachers with the resources they need and the training to implement the change well. Each teacher can experience success vicariously, meaning they see other teachers be successful with the reform. A principal can promote vicarious experiences by scheduling peer observations, recording lessons on video for others to see, and by talking about the success of teachers in the presence of the faculty.

A trustworthy principal's words carry far more weight than many realize. Teachers often crave to have feedback from principals, and during the change process, they want validation. When principals give teachers words of validation by giving them specific feedback, their efficacious beliefs increase. This source of validation is verbal persuasion.

Lastly, efficacious beliefs are affected by the way teachers feel—otherwise known as physiological factors. If the current climate of the school is negative because of frustration and stress, teachers' efficacious beliefs are likely to decrease. Reform is problematic, even in the healthiest of schools; a constant climate of negativity makes sustainable reform even more difficult to accomplish. Principals must be aware of how they talk to teachers and students, not only the words they use but *how* they voice them.

Here is an easy way to remember the four sources of efficacy: *I know I can do it* (mastery experiences); *I see that I can do it* (vicarious experiences); *I hear that I can do it* (verbal persuasion); and *I feel like I can do it* (physiological factors).

SUSTAINABILITY

Sustainability is the point at which the reform has been in place long enough to become part of the culture of the school. The teachers and students expect the change to be present—in fact, the change does not seem like a change anymore. It becomes the way things are done normally. Unfortunately, sustainability does imply change maintenance. Although the house has been built, routine checks have to be made and supplies have to be replenished.

Some of the major aspects of sustainability are reflection and adjustment. School populations and needs shift from year to year. Not only does the makeup of the school community change, but the staff members and the leadership change. The reform that has already been implemented will be molded and shaped throughout the years, depending on the needs of the school. Routine checks should be made throughout the school year using data. This can be done quickly during a leadership team meeting. Or, the principal can delegate the task of analyzing data concerning the reform to another staff member who will communicate the findings with the principal.

A yearly assessment or reevaluation of the program or initiative is important. Principals should set aside time to meet with their leadership teams to reevaluate all the programs in the school. Here are some guiding questions that one may use when deciding whether the programs or initiatives are effective:

- What programs or initiatives do we have in place?
- Does data, both qualitative and quantitative, support the need for these programs?
- Does data, both qualitative and quantitative, support the success of these programs?
- What programs/initiatives are working?
- What programs/initiatives are not working?
- What needs do we still have that are not currently being addressed?
- How can we better align our funds to continue the support of these programs/initiatives?
- What can we do to make these programs/initiatives more impactful next year?
- Are these programs/initiatives truly what our students need *right now*?

Of course, a principal should look at each program separately when answering several of the previous questions.

CASE STUDY

An elementary school on the cusp of receiving the high-performance school title applies to participate in a district initiative to transform classrooms into student-centered learning environments. Seven teachers in the faculty volunteer to participate. They receive stipends to transform their classrooms with flexible seating, and the teachers embark on planning lessons that are more rigorous and require more student autonomy. With the help of national consultants, they end their summer break by learning about what student-centered learning is.

Excited and ready to begin, these kindergarten, first-, and second-grade teachers anticipate the arrival of their students. Very quickly, the teachers are met with numerous obstacles they did not expect. In fact, they have weekly—almost daily—crying sessions with their co-workers. These high-performing teachers completely changed their practice, and it has them rethinking every decision they made over the summer.

Fortunately, their principal is extremely supportive and consistently works with them to help them through the challenges. The principal also admits that she's learning about these new strategies herself. The teachers, although extremely discouraged at the beginning of the year, rely on one another to figure out what to do next. This is part of the culture of the school—working together and relying on one another to overcome challenges.

Throughout the process, they decide, with the principal, that they want to change their school's motto to reflect the work they have accomplished and who they have become throughout the process. At the end of the first year of the initiative, the teachers are selected by the district superintendent to share their journey because of the success they have experienced. Though extremely successful, each teacher admits she has much more to learn and that she cannot wait to see how next year will unfold.

The principal and her leadership team have already discussed their plan to expand the initiative across the school, using the seven teachers to mentor others on the faculty. They listed their mistakes, challenges, and successes, and they used them to plan for the next year. Although the teachers experienced failure in the beginning, because of the leadership of the principal, the strong school culture, and the collective sense of efficacy, these teachers became successful by the end of one school year.

The case study is also an example of building capacity. Any principal who micromanages and is overly controlling is at risk for burnout. Furthermore, these types of principals can be ineffective. Strong leaders seek out those with leadership potential and begin to mentor and prepare them. These future leaders can then assist the principal by bearing some of the responsibilities, which can prepare them for future positions. The principal in the example utilized her strongest teachers by having them mentor other teachers taking on the new initiative.

Many leaders use the Managing Complex Change Model to diagnose or prevent obstacles to the change process.[10] Leaders need to ensure that five elements are present throughout the change process: vision, skills, incentives, resources, and an action plan. As the model demonstrates, lack of any key element can result in confusion, anxiety, gradual change, frustration, or false starts.

CHAPTER SUMMARY

The reader of this chapter will quickly realize that the change process is very complex. This chapter discussed ten concepts; the understanding and consideration of each play a crucial role in influencing the success or failure of strategies designed to bring about meaningful change in a school organization. Every educational leader whose goal is to initiate positive changes in his or her school must understand the following concepts:

1. *Change is a process.* Second-order change does not happen overnight. It takes time and patience.

2. *People will resist change.* Almost always, no matter how much a leader works to get his or her faculty on board, there will be some who will resist the change. Leaders must be prepared to be criticized.
3. *Moral purpose must guide the change.* People need to be invested in the change, but that does not happen unless they feel that it will affect the greater good.
4. *Preparation for change is a must.* Those who read this chapter will note that the majority of the pages were devoted to the preparation for and initiation of change. That is because it is that important! The change will fail if proper planning has not taken place.
5. *It is possible to make the change process efficient.* With proper planning, a principal can put an action plan into place that makes the change process more efficient. Transparency is the key. People usually want to know what is going to happen and why.
6. *Change will cause problems, but problems can be used to strengthen the organization.* Principals must face problems as they arise instead of waiting for the problems to dissipate. However, principals are not expected to solve problems without any help! When faculties tackle issues together, the problem-solving process often creates a stronger bond.
7. *Readiness for change often predicts the success of the change.* District and school leaders must consider the factors that greatly affect change: school culture, school climate, teacher efficacy, and collective efficacy. Sometimes the need for change can be so urgent, leaders have no choice but to enact second-order changes. However, principals must be cognizant of the impact of the previously mentioned constructs because they also affect student achievement.
8. *Mandates can produce results.* Although mandates are not recommended for second-order changes, they are useful for some first-order changes. Sometimes first-order mandates lay the groundwork for more sophisticated change. For instance, having teachers use a specific lesson plan template and creating a deadline for turning in lesson plans each week will lay the groundwork for teacher collaboration in planning. When the principal shows that he values the planning process by setting guidelines and monitoring the process, that attitude will eventually affect the teachers' perceptions of the importance of planning. Here is another example: If a principal believes that the school faculty needs to demonstrate more professionalism, which is a culture shift, she can mandate a faculty dress code to be followed at all times. Though the principal will experience resistance, over time, the teachers' mind-set changes.
9. *Changing too much causes unnecessary chaos.* As stated before, change is not a one-time event. It is a process. This is why changing

too much at one time can be disastrous. In some schools, teachers are expected to go through the change process five times with five different initiatives in one school year. Nothing is done methodically because they are asked to do too much at once. Teachers then experience confusion and frustration. Principals must work with their leadership teams to determine the focus for the year, plan for the change process, and enact it carefully.

10. *Leadership is directly related to the success or demise of the change.* A strong leader is absolutely critical to the change process. Without a clear vision and driving purpose behind the change, stakeholders are rarely able to enact the change properly. So many initiatives fall flat because the leader does not support it.

NOTES

1. Robert J. Marzano, Timothy Waters, and Brian A. McNulty, *School Leadership That Works: From Research to Results* (Heatherton, Victoria, Australia: Hawker Brownlow Education, 2006).

2. Daniel P. Johnson, *Sustaining Change in Schools: How to Overcome Differences and Focus on Quality* (Alexandria, VA: Association for Supervision and Curriculum Development, 2005).

3. Douglas Fiore, *Creating Connections for Better Schools: How Leaders Enhance School Culture* (Larchmont, NY: Eye on Education, 2001), 9.

4. Anita Woolfolk Hoy, and Wayne K. Hoy, *Instructional Leadership: A Learning-Centered Guide* (Boston: Pearson/Allyn and Bacon, 2006).

5. Kent D. Peterson and Terrence E. Deal, *The Shaping School Culture Fieldbook* (San Francisco: Jossey-Bass, 2009).

6. Albert Bandura, "Self-Efficacy: Toward a Unifying Theory of Behavioral Change," *Psychological Review* 84, no. 2 (1977): 191–215. doi:10.1037//0033-295x.84.2.191.

7. John Hattie, Proceedings of Third Annual Visible Learning Conference (subtitled "Mindframes and Maximizers"), Washington, DC, July 11–12, 2016.

8. Erin Willie Stokes, "The Development of the School Reform Model: The Impact of Critical Constructs of School Culture, School Climate, Teacher Efficacy, and Collective Efficacy on Reform" (EdD diss., University of Louisiana at Lafayette, 2016).

9. Michael Fullan, *Leading in a Culture of Change* (San Francisco: Jossey-Bass, 2001).

10. Mary Lippitt, "The Managing Complex Change Model," 1987.

Chapter Six

Systems Alignment

Amanda Shuford Mayeaux, EdD

On the front page of the Plains School District's website, the top banner read, "All successfully learning . . . all the time." Despite the proclamation, the district had been struggling with communication for many years. The district website was colorful, but elements like the calendar were often out of date. Stakeholders complained information was difficult to find. A seemingly minor issue turned into a major problem at the beginning of the school year from generic school supply lists the district had published in June on the district web page.

Meanwhile, Plains East Elementary School, the top-performing school in the district, had published specific school supply lists for each grade level on the school's website. When school began, parents who had bought the generic list were furious to find out they had bought the wrong supplies. Calls to board members followed, and the superintendent found herself in the midst of a publicity nightmare.

The following January, the district hired a new technology director, Mr. Macks. Mr. Macks was a highly efficient and well-respected technology person. He immediately formed a committee of school leaders, teachers, and parents to create an informative and well-designed district website. His team at the district office created or redesigned websites for each school. Each principal submitted one teacher's name to be the technology coordinator for each school.

These teachers were invited to attend a two-day power session where the websites were created and expectations were clearly outlined. Expectations included calendars updated each week, newsletters present on the home page of each school, and a monitoring of individual teacher websites. After websites were completed, the district technology committee analyzed and gave feedback on each site. The committee continued to monitor the site the first year and gave feedback.

After the first year, these expectations became part of the district and school cultures. Communication was aligned, and many issues were resolved from this alignment. While stating, "All successfully learning . . . all the time" is a positive phrase, modeling the sentiment day in and day out is much more powerful.

SYSTEMS ALIGNMENT

For this text, systems alignment is defined as the alignment and coherence of all the elements of a school system to not only the federal, state, and local policies governing a system, but also to the system's mission and vision statements.

Much of local school policy is dictated by federal and state laws. Compliance requires constant monitoring and reassessment of local policies as new policies regularly trickle down to the district and school levels. Policy is required to be aligned with various mandates, but often an additional element is simply tacked onto an already existing program to create the illusion of alignment. Strong school and district leaders have the skills and knowledge to research and understand complicated laws, in order to create solid alignment, which may include eliminating existing programs or structures to modifying existing programs.

The second type of alignment, which is often ignored, is the alignment of policy to the mission and vision statements. These statements are traditionally found in handbooks and on signs around schools and district, but districts and schools do not consider how policy aligns to the stated mission and vision. These statements are the "talk" and should be aligned to the "walk." In successful districts and schools, the "talk" is strongly aligned to the "walk."[1]

IMPORTANCE AND SIGNIFICANCE OF SYSTEMS ALIGNMENT TO FEDERAL AND STATE LAW

Systems alignment to federal and state law pertains to a wide range of areas. Most commonly, the focus is on curricular and performance alignment. Since the inception of No Child Left Behind in 2002, the federal government has become increasingly involved in shaping state and district policy in the areas of curriculum, instruction, and assessment. NCLB introduced mandates that required states to meet through the alignment of teacher certification and assessments. This shift embedded the federal government much more heavily in the instructional aspect of schools.

Mandates from curriculum to assessment to teacher qualifications change with shifts in administrations and political winds. The difficulty for schools and districts is aligning systems in an efficient and effective manner. The other issue is that often mandates run crossways to already existing programs, which impacts personnel and fiscal policies. Changing these policies to meet the mandates requires political buy-in from district boards. Having a system in place to analyze and evaluate the requirement of the new mandates in order to decide how to successfully implement these mandates is a critical task for district and school leaders.

EVALUATING ALIGNMENT TO SCHOOL AND DISTRICT POLICIES AND PROCEDURES

Evaluation of the alignment of school and district policies and procedures can be complicated and politically difficult. Having a clearly defined process can increase transparency and effectiveness. Some steps a district and/or school may take in analyzing and evaluation policy alignment include the following:

1. Clearly dissect the policy:

   - What are the specific requirements of the policy?
   - Who does this policy specifically impact?
   - Who should be part of the implementation planning team?
   - What is the timeline for the implementation of the policy?
   - What is the financial impact of the policy?
   - What existing programs does this policy impact? Is the impact positive or negative?

2. Analyze the policy for impact:

   - How will the implementation of this policy impact students?
   - How will the implementation of this policy impact schools?
   - How will the implementation of this policy impact personnel?
   - How will the implementation impact the district as a whole?
   - What district/school goals does this policy impact?

3. Create an implementation plan:

   - What is the overall implementation plan (pilot school vs. full district)?
   - What specific steps do we need to take to implement this policy?
   - What current programs/systems support this policy?

- What current programs/systems contradict this policy?
- How do we solve the conflicts?
- What is the implementation timeline?
- Who are the stakeholders in the implementation?
- How do we educate stakeholders?
- What is the human resource impact (hires vs. reassigning, training needed, etc.)?
- What fiscal requirements are needed?
- What is the budget for this implementation?
- Who will monitor the implementation?
- How will we monitor compliance?
- What defines successful compliance?
- How will we make adjustments?

4. Implement and monitor the plan. Here are the checkpoint requirements:

   - Who will monitor implementation?
   - How will the implementation be monitored?
   - What reports are expected?
   - When will reports be shared?

5. Refine the plan:

   - When will refinements (if needed) be made?
   - Who will make decisions about the refinements?

WORKING THE PROCESS

For example, the Plains School District's state mandated all schools to increase opportunities for all students to earn college credit, including dual-enrollment and vocational credit, while in high school. The state added an accountability component to encourage districts to comply. The Plains School District formed a team of high school principals, counselors, teachers, and parents to analyze the mandate and create a plan to present to the school board.

Clearly Dissect the Policy

The specific requirements of the policy stated all students would be offered postsecondary opportunities including dual-enrollment courses and/or vocational credit courses. The policy was passed in June and expected to be implemented at the beginning of school in September, but accountability measures would begin counting for the incoming freshman class.

The accountability carrot dangled in front of schools was the addition of points per student for each course earned. Students earning an associate's degree prior to high school graduation and/or a hire wage/high-demand certification earned the school maximum points. The requirements of the policy did not define how the schools would meet the expectations but did offer additional funding of $100 per student (K–12) in the district to support the mandate.

Analyze the Policy for Impact

The policy impacted high school students directly, but middle school students would also be impacted as in order to meet the goal of juniors and seniors taking postsecondary coursework, some of the high school courses would have to shift to middle school. Teachers would also be impacted as certification issues would have to be explored and each teacher's certification at each middle school would have to be examined to see where high school courses could be taught. Additionally, if juniors and seniors began taking college courses, some high school teachers could be displaced or need additional training in order to teach new courses.

The team decided the first step would be to run a financial needs analysis and assigned researching cost to the high school director and her team. After a week, the cost was determined to be an additional $500 per junior and senior for only courses and materials. The offset of the state money would cover the program, but the team had additional concerns about possible transportation costs and administrative costs.

The team decided the policy would have a negative impact on the growing AP courses offered in the high school and also worried the policy would move students further into college-bound versus vocational tracks. The team decided to one goal would be to offer a bilevel program where students could earn both an associate's degree and an industry-based certification. The positive impact would be that students would leave the high schools with college credits, which saved parents money once students entered college, and/or an industry-based certification, which allowed students to enter the job force out of high school.

Plains School District set three goals for the initial implementation:

1. A minimum of 60 percent of high school juniors and seniors would participate in and pass offered college-level and/or industry-based course opportunities.
2. All freshmen and sophomores would be given additional support through their core courses to be eligible for coursework in their junior

and senior year. An emphasis would be placed upon ACT and ACT-WorkKeys skills. ACT would also be offered to sophomores.
3. The district would hire and/or train twenty teachers to be eligible to provide dual-enrollment courses at the high school.

Create an Implementation Plan

The district moved one of the assistant principals, Mr. Jones, from Plains High School to a district position to manage the implementation of the plan. Mr. Jones would report to the high school director and would host weekly meetings with the central office team. The team outlined immediate steps for implementation for the upcoming school year and a separate implementation plan for the future. The plan was presented to the board and passed in early July.

Mr. Jones began working with school counselors to contact parents and students about the new course opportunities. Mr. Jones worked with the local community college to create course opportunities, enroll students, register students for courses, and provide all required documentation. For vocational courses, Mr. Jones worked with the technical and career director, Mrs. Smith, to match instructors with courses.

Some instructors required additional training, which Mrs. Smith added to her budget. The cafeteria manager worked with each school counselor to solve food program issues for students who might leave early to go to the college for courses. Mr. Jones and the transportation director created a system for the bus to provide transportation to the college for students who did not drive. For those who did drive, the parents were required to provide legal permission and insurance information. The first few weeks of the fall were bumpy, but Mr. Jones and the team worked through issues, and by December the policy was working fairly well.

Conflicts began to arise when teachers and principals realized the policy potentially displaced teachers and impacted extracurricular activities from sports to homecoming. Students who were not on campus were unavailable to participate in things like pep rallies and other activities. The fine arts high school saw a dramatic drop in students available to take music, arts, and theater courses because of timing issues.

The principal, whose husband was the elementary director, began to encourage students to not take the college courses in order to "save" her fine arts programs. Mr. Jones met with the school team several times without solution. Finally, the high school director and superintendent became involved and a compromise was met. The teachers with advanced degrees in their fields would be certified by the community college to teach fine arts college-level courses at the school. The schedule would be changed so juniors and seniors would take fine arts courses in the morning and be free to take college courses in the afternoon.

The high schools began working with freshmen and sophomores to prepare them for future course expansion, and middle schools began teaching three new high school courses at the middle school level. Mr. Jones worked with each school to create parent information nights throughout the fall and spring.

Implement and Monitor the Plan

Each week Mr. Jones met with the two directors to discuss progress. Once a month this small team reported to the superintendent and submitted a report to the board and to the principals. The team also submitted public updates via the district website each month.

Refine the Plan

After the fall semester, adjustments were made to increase the course offerings, including some night courses for seniors, who provided their own transportation, and additional virtual courses, which could be taken at the high schools. In the spring, the board voted to create an early college model on the community college campus in addition to the increasing the course options taught on the high school campuses. The team also contracted with a local agency to provide a wider array of vocational courses. Mrs. Smith managed these courses, and a principal was hired to create and develop the early college.

The financial burden had a negative impact on the budget. The board increased the funding to the program. Mrs. Smith added additional dollars by eliminating a hospitality program, which was not producing results, to support the increase in vocational students in welding. Mr. Jones convinced principals to provide textbooks, and the parents were asked to pay the registration fees for the community college.

Honest Evaluation and Elimination of Pet Projects

Often the issues impacting such implementation of a new policy are the lack of honest evaluation of current policies and the fear of the elimination of pet projects. Often new mandates appear to require new funding, but an unbiased examination will offer options to use resources more effectively.[2]

In Plains School District, the fine arts high school was a popular option for students. The high school culture was strong, and many students excelled. Unfortunately, despite the wonderful culture of the fine arts program, the school focus did not meet the state expectations for students. Having a structure to clearly analyze and evaluate policy assists in transparency and wrangling of political hot topics. Pet projects and programs not making an impact have to be clearly examined and discussed without feelings, emotions, and politics impacting decisions about what would be best for students.

No policy implementation works perfectly the first time, but having an implementation plan with monitoring and refinement steps integrated makes quicker success possible.

IMPORTANCE OF SYSTEMS ALIGNMENT TO THE MISSION AND VISION

The mission and vision statements should be the central part of a school system's beliefs. Strong alignment occurs when leaders and policy makers apply these belief statements as the foundation when making choices and decisions, rather than the ever-changing choices to meet political whims. Too often schools and districts find themselves in opposition to what they claim to believe. Throughout this chapter, we will examine what strong alignment should be.

Culture and climate are critical elements in the success of a school and a district. Often leadership attempts to improve the culture and the climate by enacting new campaigns and adding catchy slogans. Banners are created and placed all around the schools in the district. Flower beds are added. Teachers and staff are given T-shirts, and everyone is excited about the movement to a more positive outlook. However, soon these changes begin to fall away, and the old habits and attitudes begin to emerge. The walk is not matching the talk. How does this happen? What can be done to positively change culture and climate? The most crucial step is for every word, every decision, and every action to be aligned to what districts and schools say we believe.

Plains School District claimed the following statements:

- Vision Statement: All successfully learning . . . all the time.
- Mission Statement: Plains School District nurtures and supports all learners to develop their skills, knowledge, and competencies to be productive citizens in our local community and competitive in a constantly changing global economy.

Plains School District said they consider all stakeholders as learners and their schools to be the nucleus of the learning. Notice the words "to be" has been used as opposed "to become" in the mission statement. These simple two words demonstrate the district's belief that students, teachers, leaders, and all stakeholders are currently engaged in the local and global community. The mission is to build upon what is currently happening and improve skills, knowledge, and competencies. While this element may seem minor, the focus on using current skills, knowledge, and competencies to build toward the future signals an optimistic culture where the stakeholders see their strengths as foundation toward success.

Examples of the mismatch in alignment are prevalent in many districts and schools. One example would be a school where the claim is that student learning is the focus—"All successfully learning . . . all the time"—but the office consistently interrupts classroom instruction with announcements throughout the day. Another simple example would be one where a school claims that professional learning is part of the "All successfully learning . . . all the time," but teachers are pulled during their professional learning time to substitute in another teacher's classroom. These are small examples, but when these types of issues occur over and over, the misalignment begins to erode the culture and climate of the school.

EXAMINING ALIGNMENT TO THE MISSION AND VISION STATEMENTS

Alignment is the critical evidence that a school and district believe what they claim to believe. As with analyzing and evaluating policy alignment, the analysis of systems alignment to the mission and vision statements is transparent when clearly defined steps are used.

1. Dissect each program for impact:

   - What are the specific elements of the program?
   - What is the history of this program?
   - What mandates does this program satisfy?

2. Analyze the policy for impact:

   - How does this program specifically impact students?
   - Is the impact positive or negative? What is the specific evidence? (Data may be quantitative and qualitative)
   - What is the financial impact of the program?
   - How does this program impact the budget?
   - How does this program impact personnel?

NEXT STEPS

Does this program align to the mission and vision statements? What is the clear and specific evidence? If yes, how can the alignment be clearly and consistently communicated to all stakeholders? If no, can the program be modified to align to the mission and vision statements? What is the clear and indefensible evidence? If no, the program is eliminated. If eliminated, what will be the impact on students, schools, teachers, and other personnel?

THE ALIGNMENT DISCUSSION

The superintendent, Dr. Simpson, had been serving in Plains School District for five years. On the outside, the district was fairly successful with several high-performing schools and three schools slowly improving. The strength of the district was the teaching and learning occurring in the schools. The superintendent had cultivated a strong district instructional team, and most of the schools were led by strong instructional leaders.

The most difficult issue Dr. Simpson dealt with was the school board and the undercurrent of politics, which often derailed innovations and ideas, particularly in noninstructional issues. Frustrated with the constant backstabbing and difficulty in having the board come to consensus, Dr. Simpson decided to use the alignment analysis and evaluation process with the board.

Dr. Simpson gave the board the task of analyzing the alignment of various elements of the district. He thought this might be key to overcoming the behind-the-scenes politics to push the system forward. Each of the ten board members was assigned a partner from the central office, plus a school administrator and a teacher leader. The task was to review the assigned areas for alignment with the vision and mission statements of the district. The committees were as follows: (1) financial, (2) human resources, (3) special services, (4) extracurricular, and (5) auxiliary services. If a misalignment was found, the team was asked to make a suggestion for realigning the issue to match the mission.

- Vision Statement: All successfully learning . . . all the time.
- Mission Statement: Plains School District nurtures and supports all learners to develop their skills, knowledge, and competencies to be productive citizens in our local community and competitive in a constantly changing global economy.

The groups spent two days during the summer retreat analyzing various choices and policies for alignment. The results were astounding, and misalignment issues emerged in each category.

The financial committee noted several discrepancies in the way the money was spent compared to the mission statement's words "nurtures and supports all learners to develop." One school, in particular, had received the majority of the technology budget over the past five years. A board member's wife was the principal of the school, which had been noted in quiet conversations but not publicly addressed. In the principal's defense, her staff was proficient in writing grants and often participated in the writing of the technology grants. However, to have one school so far and above the other schools in resources did not align with the mission statement.

The group recommended two actions: (1) host a grant writing seminar for the district where the outstanding grant writers from the school could share their wisdom, and (2) create a systemic plan to have all schools equally funded and equipped by the end of two years.

Human resources found a misalignment in the placement of career and technical education teachers to the mission statement's promise the students would be globally competitive. The district had attempted to offer more technical certification opportunities to secondary students. The certifications were useful in the surrounding industries as gateways to better jobs. Unfortunately, with the retirement of many technical teachers, the district had been unable to fill the positions. The team had brainstormed and shared new ideas for recruiting technical teachers, including creating partnerships with the community college and technical companies in the area. Human resources made this their target goal for the year.

The special services group found many misalignments, but the most critical one was the lack of support services for the students who were classified as emotionally disabled. The misalignment to "All successfully learning . . . all the time" was not only for the special needs students, but also for the other students whom the outbursts were impacting. In three incidents from the previous year, other students had been harmed from an emotionally disturbed student's outbursts. Additionally, one teacher had been placed on disability after being beaten by a student. The number of students requiring these services had grown rapidly in the past five years without anyone tracking the possible reasons why.

These students needed specific interventions, in which most special education teachers were not trained. The group suggested the district recruit special education teachers willing to receive additional training to work with these students and also increase the number of counselors the schools had by forming a partnership with the local university's counseling department. The group also suggested a reassessment of how the students were placed and where.

The team focused on extracurricular activities found a complete misalignment with the finances used to support athletics in the schools versus other extracurricular activities. The misalignment focused on the word "all" found in the vision and mission statements. The funding formula was not consistent, with athletics receiving double per-pupil dollars to what other activities received. Compounding the issues was athletics was generating its own funding on top of the district support. The team suggested creating an equalizing formula to be used in all extracurricular decisions, thus removing the political sway many board members had in equipping their favorite teams.

The auxiliary services team was the team with the most recommendations. Transportation had consistently held too much power in the district. The cost of running buses, maintaining buses, and placating bus drivers had become difficult. One issue was the transportation supervisor was often unreliable and difficult to contact. Buses were often late or required leaving early from school because of needing to double up runs to cover for a missing driver. This caused a misalignment, because students were missing class time.

The team recommended clear policies be put into place for the supervisor and all working in transportation until other options could be researched. The team also recommended exploring the option of privatizing the transportation. Similarly, the team found issues in food services. There were instances where the same schools had the same issues in their cafeterias, such as running out of food, sanitation citations, and workers not going to work. The district had hired a new district supervisor the previous year and she had offered many suggestions, but politics had prevented changes. The team recommended that the supervisor be given the power to make changes and correct issues the following year with monthly check-ins with the superintendent.

CHAPTER SUMMARY

While federal and state laws dictate the majority of school and district actions, strong alignment builds culture through transparency and accountability. Systems alignment, like all the other organizational processes, requires teamwork. The systems alignment must involve collaboration and cooperation of teacher leaders and school administrators. Systems alignment cannot be accomplished in isolation and addressed by an individual, for example, the principal or his or her designee. It is only through a group process involving the input from members of all levels of an organization, teacher leaders, and administration that any process can be successful.

When districts and schools monitor and consistently assess the impact of local policies and programs to the alignment of the mission and vision statements, students benefit. Strong school and district leaders have the ability to create cohesion and transparency, in order to grow districts and implement mandates with fidelity. Strong leaders not only "talk the talk" but model the "walk" in every action and conversation.

NOTES

1. Alan M. Blankstein, *Failure Is Not an Option: Six Principles That Guide Student Achievement in High-Performing Schools* (Thousand Oaks, CA: Corwin, 2004); G. Sue Shannon and Pete Bylsma, *The Nine Characteristics of High-Performing Schools: A Research-*

Based Resource for Schools and Districts to Assist with Improving Student Learning, 2nd ed. (Olympia, WA: Office of Superintendent of Public Instruction, 2007).

2. W. Norton Grubb, "Correcting the Money Myth: Re-thinking School Resources," *Phi Delta Kappan* 91, no. 4 (2009–2010): 51–55.

Chapter Seven

School Leadership and the Law

A Field Guide for Instructional Leaders

Richard Fossey, JD, and Nathan Roberts, JD, PhD

As any school leader can attest, public education is heavily entwined with legal issues. In most states, school districts are legally required to administer regular testing to determine whether students are being adequately instructed.

Teachers and other school employees have statutory rights under both state and federal law, and they have constitutional rights as well. In addition, school districts are constrained by a web of state and federal laws that forbid school leaders from discriminating against students or school employees. Students with disabilities have legal rights guaranteed by federal statutes; and in some states, school districts have legal obligations to engage in collective bargaining with their instructional and noninstructional employees.

Obviously, this chapter cannot cover all the legal issues that impact school leaders. Nor can it address legal issues that are specific to particular states. Instead this chapter will provide a broad overview of these federal and constitutional issues:

1. Students' constitutional rights, including their right to due process and free speech, and their right to be free from unreasonable searches and seizures under the Fourth Amendment
2. Students' rights under IDEIA and a free appropriate public education
3. School employees' constitutional rights, including their right to due process, free speech, and right to be free from unreasonable searches
4. The rights of school employees and students to be free from sexual discrimination and sexual harassment as set for in Title IX of the Education Amendments of 1972.

This chapter will also provide an overview of legal issues pertaining to prayer and religious expression in schools and a short review of legal issues concerning corporal punishment of students, which will only be applicable to instructional leaders who work in the twenty-two states that authorize or permit the physical discipline of students. Finally, this chapter will briefly discuss the legal obligations of school authorities to comply with the Family Educational Rights and Privacy Act (FERPA).

STUDENTS' CONSTITUTIONAL RIGHTS

At the beginning of the twentieth century, schools had no constitutional obligations to their students that had been recognized by the courts. Educators were said to be in an in loco parentis relationship with their students—virtually the same relationship that parents had over their children.

Students' Constitutional Right to Free Speech

In 1971, however, the U.S. Supreme Court decided the case of *Tinker v. Des Moines Community School District* and ruled that students have constitutional rights that they do not relinquish when they enter through the schoolhouse gate. In particular, students enjoyed the right to free speech. "It can hardly be argued," the court said, "that either students or teachers shed their constitutional right to freedom of speech or expression at the schoolhouse gate" (p. 506).

Unless school officials reasonably forecast that a student's speech would "materially and substantially disrupt the work and discipline of the school" or interfere with the rights of other students, they must tolerate student speech (p. 513).

In subsequent opinions, the court recognized some limits on students' free speech rights. In *Bethel School District v. Fraser* (1986), the court ruled that school authorities could censor student speech that was vulgar, lewd, or sexually suggestive; and in *Morse v. Frederick* (2007), the court held that school officials could punish speech that promotes or celebrates the illegal use of drugs.

In *Hazelwood School District v. Kuhlmeier* (1988), the Supreme Court ruled that educators can censor student speech that is sponsored by the school. In that case, the court said, "Educators do not offend the First Amendment by exercising editorial control over the style and content of student speech in school-sponsored expressive activities so long as their actions are reasonably related to legitimate pedagogical concerns" (p. 273). The court specifically ruled that a school principal could censor student-written articles in the school's newspaper, which was a school-sponsored publication.

In recent years, a substantial amount of litigation has been devoted to disputes about schools' authority to punish students who express themselves through social media while off the school grounds. In general, courts have made clear that school administrators may not punish students for their social media expressions unless they can show that the speech disrupts or is likely to disrupt the work of the school.

On the other hand, an important decision by the Fourth Circuit Court of Appeals upheld discipline of a student for creating a Facebook discussion site that was devoted to ridiculing a fellow student. Such speech, the Fourth Circuit reasonably concluded, violated the school's policy against bullying and harassment and interfered with the victim's right to get an education (*Kowalski v. Berkeley County Schools*, 2011).

Students' Constitutional Right to Be Free from Unreasonable Searches and Seizures

Students also enjoy a constitutional right to be free from unreasonable searches and seizures while they are at school. In the seminal decision of *New Jersey v. TLO* (1985), the Supreme Court ruled that school administrators are not required to obtain a warrant before searching a student or the student's personal belongings. Nor are school administrators bound by the "probable cause" standard that applies to police searches.

They are, however, required to conduct student searches under a two-part reasonableness standard, which requires school officials to show that a search is both reasonable at its inception and reasonable in scope. A search will be reasonable at its inception, the court instructed, "when there are reasonable grounds for suspecting that the search will turn up evidence that the student has violated or is violating the law or the rules of the school." A search will be found reasonable in scope "when the measures adopted are reasonably related to the objectives of the search and not excessively intrusive in light of the age and sex of the student and the nature of the infraction" (p. 342).

In the years following the *TLO* decision, schools have experienced considerable litigation over student searches, with most disputes arising from searches for drugs, weapons, or other contraband. In general, the courts have deferred to administrative decisions to search students or their possessions when school officials can articulate a reasonable basis for commencing a search and when the search itself is not offensive to a student's privacy or dignity. The courts have been consistently hostile, however, to strip searches, which the Supreme Court defined as searches that require students to disrobe to their underwear (*Safford Unified School District v. Redding*, 2009).

The Supreme Court has ruled that a drug test involving the extraction of bodily fluids constitutes a search under the Fourth Amendment if conducted by government officials, and the court has spoken twice with regard to urine testing of students by school authorities.

In *Vernonia School District 437J v. Acton* (1995), the court upheld the constitutionality of a school policy calling for random drug testing of student athletes. Such searches did not require a warrant, the court reasoned, because school officials had a special need to ensure that student athletes were not using illegal drugs and student athletes had a diminished expectation of privacy when participating in varsity athletics. Moreover, the school's drug-testing program was not conducted for the purpose of criminal prosecution and test results were not shared with police.

In a later decision, the court expanded on its decision in *Acton* and ruled that schools can require all students participating in any school-sponsored extracurricular activity to submit to drug testing by urinalysis (*Board of Education of Independent School District No. 92 of Pottawatomie County v. Earls*, 2002). Moreover, school authorities were not required to establish they had a serious problem with student drug abuse as a condition of implementing a student drug-testing program.

Students' Right to Procedural Due Process

Students also enjoy a constitutional right to procedural due process before they are expelled or suspended from school. In *Goss v. Lopez*, decided in 1975, the Supreme Court ruled that students are entitled to at least the rudiments of procedural due process before being suspended for even a short period of time—ten days or less. In such circumstances, the court instructed, school officials must notify the student either orally or in writing of the grounds for discipline and give the student an opportunity to rebut the charges.

Such informal hearings need not be lengthy and can be postponed if the student is so disruptive that the hearing cannot take place immediately. Nevertheless, school officials cannot dispense with due process concerns altogether, even when the student discipline involves only a short out-of-school suspension.

Although the Supreme Court has not spelled out the parameters of procedural due process for lengthier suspensions or expulsions, it is generally agreed that long-term suspensions require a more formal due process hearing where a student can cross-examine witnesses and present evidence (*Dixon v. Alabama State Board of Education*, 1961). In many states, the procedural requirements for expelling a student are set forth in statutes.

Student Rights under IDEIA

Instructional leaders work daily with students who are covered by the Individuals with Disabilities Education Improvement Act of 2004 (IDEIA, P.L. 108-446, 2004). Disputes between school districts and parents regarding special education is common; thus, it is necessary that school leaders understand and fairly administer the legal rights of disabled children and their parents. IDEIA's goal is to provide that all children with disabilities have available to them a free and appropriate public education (FAPE) that focuses on special education services designed to meet their unique needs.

A major component of FAPE is to ensure that to the maximum extent possible students with disabilities are educated with other students who are not disabled, in the least restrictive environment.

Normally, the components of an appropriate public education are delineated in the Individualized Education Program (IEP). This program highlights the educational services and provides an avenue for parent involvement. The IEP team that develops the program is generally composed of a general education teacher, a special education teacher, a local education agency representative (LEA), a person to interpret evaluation results, and the student's parents. The U.S. Supreme Court in *Board of Education of Hendrick Hudson Central School District v. Rowley* (1982) established what qualifies as FAPE.

The court ruled the law was not designed to provide services to maximize each student's potential. Instead, the law was to provide access to a free public education that provided a floor of opportunity that consists of individualized specialized instruction and related services designed to create an educational benefit to the student. In 2017, the court in *Endrew F. v. Douglas County School District* modified the *Rowley* de minimis standard and raised it to require a program reasonably calculated to enable a child to make progress appropriate in light of the child's circumstance.

Related and supplemental services involve transportation and supportive services such as speech-language pathology and audiology services, and counseling and medical services that are necessary for a disabled student to benefit from the special education program. Medical services must be provided if necessary for the student to remain in school during the day except those services that can only be provided by a physician (*Irving Independent School District v. Tatro*, 1984). If the services must be provided to the student to remain in school, the school district must fund the related services to guarantee the student can participate in public school (*Cedar Rapids Community School District v. Garret F.*, 1999).

Special education students are entitled to certain procedural due process safeguards to ensure students with disabilities the necessary benefits and appropriate services. For example, all parents must receive written notice of their rights, as outlined in Section 615 (d)(1)(A)(i–iii). If disagreements occur between parents and school districts, parents are entitled to a due process hearing to challenge the districts position.

States must provide mediation services at state cost, and impartial hearing officers are available to hear evidence presented by both sides. Either party may appeal a due process finding to state or federal court, as in Section 615 (f). Courts then have the authority to grant appropriate relief including changes in placement, additional services, and reimbursement of expenses. During the pendency of either mediation or due process hearings, the student remains in the current educational placement unless the parent and the LEA agree to a change in placement for the student.

Finally, IDEIA provides a balancing mechanism between the need for discipline and safety at school and the rights of disabled students. Disciplinary procedures are set forth in Section 615 (k)(1)(A–D) providing a case-by-case analysis of student discipline issues to determine if the discipline issue is a manifestation of the student's disability. If it is not related to the student's disability, the student may be disciplined the same as other students; however, services must be continued. If a student is removed from his or her placement for more than ten school days, the student must receive a functional behavioral assessment and behavioral intervention services to address the behavior.

CONSTITUTIONAL RIGHTS OF SCHOOL EMPLOYEES

Public school teachers and other school employees enjoy certain constitutional rights, including the constitutional right to free speech and due process and the right to be free from unreasonable searches and seizures. In most school districts, school administrators can rely on state statutes and formal policies to guide them concerning their constitutional duties, since most statutes and policies will conform to constitutional standards. For example, most states spell out the procedural rules for terminating tenured and nontenured teachers in state statutes, and these statutes will almost always comply with constitutional requirements of procedural due process.

Free Speech Rights of Public Employees

Public employees, including public school teachers, enjoy a constitutional right to free speech, but courts have weighed that right against the legitimate interests that public employers have in harmony and efficiency in the workplace. In *Pickering v. Board of Education* (1968), the leading case on public employees' free speech rights, the Supreme Court articulated a constitutional rule that has come to be known as the *Pickering* balancing test. "The problem in any case," the court articulated, "is to arrive at a balance between the interests of the teacher, as citizen, in commenting on matters of public concern and the interests of the State, as an employer, in promoting the efficiency of the public services it performs through its employees" (p. 568).

In *Pickering*, an Illinois schoolteacher published a letter in a local newspaper that criticized some of his employing school board's financial decisions. The school board fired him over the letter, which the board maintained was inaccurate and "detrimental to the efficient operation and administration of the schools of the district" (p. 564). Pickering sued, and the dismissal was upheld by the Illinois Supreme Court.

On appeal to the U.S. Supreme Court, the Illinois court's decision was reversed. The U.S. Supreme Court concluded that Pickering's letter addressed a matter of legitimate public concern and had not disrupted school operations or impeded Pickering in the performance of his teaching duties. "In these circumstances," the Supreme Court ruled, "we conclude that the interest of the school administration in limiting teachers' opportunities to contribute to public debate is not significantly greater than its interest in limiting a similar contribution by any member of the general public" (p. 573).

After all, the court noted, "Teachers are, as a class, the members of a community most likely to have informed and definite opinions as to how funds allotted to the operation of the schools should be spent" (p. 572).

Although teachers have a broad right to speak as citizens on matters of public concern, those rights are severely restricted when a teacher speaks in an official capacity as a school employee. In *Garcetti v. Ceballos* (2006), the Supreme Court ruled that public employees enjoy no First Amendment protection for speech made pursuant to their job duties. Several federal courts have applied *Garcetti* in the school context and have ruled that teachers essentially have no First Amendment protection when they are speaking in their official capacity as school employees (*Brown v. Chicago Board of Education*, 2016; *Evans-Marshall v. Tipp City Exempted Village School District*, 2010; *Williams v. Dallas Independent School District*, 2007.

Nor do public school teachers have an academic freedom right that protects their teaching style or their curricular decisions. The school curriculum is school-sponsored speech, and school authorities may censor teacher expression in the learning environment (*Miles v. Denver Public Schools*, 1991). Moreover, a teacher has no constitutional or academic-freedom right to utilize curricular materials that are not approved by the school board (*Evans-Marshall v. Tipp City Exempted Village School District*, 2010).

A teacher's minimal constitutional protection for classroom speech was dramatically emphasized in *Brown v. Chicago Board of Education* (2016), in which a teacher was disciplined for using the n-word as part of an informal and impromptu exhortation to students not to use the word. The Sixth Circuit expressed skepticism about the wisdom of punishing a teacher who was obviously attempting to promote civic speech in the classroom. Nevertheless, the court was bound by judicial precedent and upheld the school board's disciplinary decision.

School administrators who occupy confidential or policy-making positions are more restricted regarding their constitutional right to criticize policy decisions by their employers. In *Dixon v. University of Toledo* (2012), for example, a public university fired a senior administrator after she published an op-ed essay in a local newspaper criticizing the university's policy regarding health care benefits for same-sex couples. The firing decision was upheld by the Sixth Circuit Court of Appeals, which ruled that the university's interest in efficiency outweighed a policy-making administrator's right to publicly criticize a university policy.

Similarly, a school administrator who takes an active role in school board elections and whose candidate is defeated has no First Amendment right to keep his job if an antagonistic relationship develops between the superintendent and the school board majority. In *Kinsey v. Salado Independent School District* (1992), the Fifth Circuit Court of Appeals ruled that a superintendent had the power to "make or break" board policies and that "a close working relationship" between school board members and the school superintendent is essential.

Thus, the superintendent's "right to speech or political opposition to a majority of the officials elected by the community to govern him is outweighed by the board's legitimate interest in having a superintendent with loyalty to the new board's policies and directives" (p. 992, emphasis by the court).

School boards sometimes discipline or even terminate an employee for a variety of reasons, including displeasure about a teacher's constitutionally protected speech. Does a teacher have the right to avoid discipline when the school board's decision has mixed motivations?

In *Mt. Healthy City School District v. Doyle* (1977), the Supreme Court answered this question. In *Doyle*, a school board decided to terminate a nontenured teacher for a variety of deficiencies, which the board listed in writing. Among the board's concerns was an incident in which Doyle had gotten into an argument with cafeteria workers over the amount of spaghetti that he was served. Doyle had also gotten into an argument with another teacher that culminated in the other teacher slapping him. In addition, Doyle had described students as "sons of bitches" in a disciplinary complaint and made an obscene gesture toward two girls who failed to comply with his directives.

None of these incidents had any apparent First Amendment implications, but the school board was also motivated not to renew Doyle's contract because he had called a radio station and complained about a memorandum distributed by Doyle's principal concerning teacher dress and appearance. In a federal district court's view, Doyle's communication with the radio station was constitutionally protected speech, and therefore the school board's decision not to renew Doyle's contract, which was based partly on an unconstitutional motivation, required the decision to be nullified on First Amendment grounds.

On appeal to the U.S. Supreme Court, the district court's decision was vacated with directions to consider the case again in accordance with guidance laid down by the Supreme Court. According to the court, Doyle had the initial burden of showing he had engaged in constitutionally protected conduct and that this conduct formed a "substantial factor" in the school board's decision to terminate him. Once Doyle met his burden of proof, the Supreme Court instructed, the school board then had the burden of showing by a preponderance of the evidence "that it would have reached the same decision as to respondent's reemployment even in the absence of the [constitutionally] protected conduct" (p. 287).

In sum, the district court was directed to determine whether the school board would have made the same decision to terminate Doyle's employment even if he had not made a phone call to the radio station. If the answer to that question is affirmative, then the board's decision must be upheld.

As the Supreme Court explained:

> A borderline or marginal candidate should not have the employment question resolved against him because of constitutionally protected conduct. But that same candidate ought not to be able, by engaging in such conduct, to prevent his employer from assessing his performance record and reaching a decision not to rehire on the basis of that record, simply because the protected conduct makes the employer more certain of the correctness of its decision. (p. 286)

Mt. Healthy City School District v. Doyle should serve as a reminder to school officials not to articulate a reason for disciplining a teacher that even arguably can be linked to constitutionally protected speech or conduct. The Mt. Healthy School Board had ample grounds for not renewing Doyle's teaching contract based on incidents that had no First Amendment implications. It erred when it listed Doyle's telephone conversation with a radio station as one of the reasons for terminating Doyle's employment.

Teachers' Right to Freedom from Unreasonable Searches and Seizures

Like students, teachers enjoy a constitutional right to freedom from unreasonable searches and seizures in the school environment. Unlike students, however, who have litigated hundreds of cases involving searches by school authorities, there is very little case law involving the search of a teacher's person or possessions by school administrators. There are, after all, very few circumstances in which a school administrator would be justified in searching a teacher or a teacher's personal belongings.

In *Shaul v. Cherry Valley–Springfield Central School District* (2004), a teacher who had been placed on administrative leave based on allegations of sexual misconduct challenged an investigative search of his classroom and a locked storage cabinet. The Second Circuit Court of Appeals affirmed a lower court's summary judgment in favor of the school district, finding no constitutional infirmities in the school administrators' conduct and ruling as follows:

> In sum, we agree with the district court that defendants were entitled to summary judgment on Shaul's claim of unreasonable search and seizure of his property on January 30, 1999. Whatever reasonable expectations of privacy Shaul may have had in personal property maintained in his classroom while he was a teacher in good standing, that expectation ended when, after being suspended for professional misconduct and barred from his classroom, he surrendered all school keys, including a key to a locked file cabinet in his classroom, at the same time that he failed to avail himself of an opportunity to retrieve his personal belongings. To the extent Shaul complains that defendants did not give him enough time to remove all his belongings on a subsequent occasion, we hold that even if that were the case, by January 30th defendants had reasonable investigatory and non-investigatory grounds for searching the classroom and removing plaintiff's personal property so that a new teacher could complete the school year. (pp. 184–185)

In essence, the Second Circuit ruled that the teacher had no expectation of privacy over his personal property in his classroom after he was suspended and had turned over his school keys. To the extent, he retained a reasonable expectation of privacy over his personal possessions, school administrators had reasonable investigatory and noninvestigatory grounds for conducting their search. The court's articulation of a reasonableness standard in the *Shaul* case is very similar to the reasonableness standard spelled out by the Supreme Court in *New Jersey v. TLO* for student searches.

In a more recent unpublished decision, the Ninth Circuit Court of Appeals ruled that a teacher had no reasonable expectation of privacy over his classroom or a desk drawer because he knew his classroom was subject to canine searches from time to time for guns, drugs, or other contraband.

Moreover, assuming arguendo that the teacher had a reasonable expectation of privacy over his desk drawer, the search of his desk drawer was reasonable after a search dog alerted authorities that there might be contraband in the drawer. Thus, the teacher's arrest for bringing a gun and knife to school did not violate his Fourth Amendment rights (*Khachatourian v. Hacienda La Puente Unified School District*, 2014).

Some school districts have policies for conducting suspicionless drug testing of school employees, including teachers, bus drivers, and school custodians. School-bus drivers are generally considered to be school employees in safety-sensitive positions, and school authorities routinely subject bus drivers to random and suspicionless testing. Drug testing of school-bus drivers is governed by federal regulations (*Anderson v. Independent School District*, 2004).

The District of Columbia Circuit Court of Appeals upheld a school district's mandatory drug testing of school-bus drivers against a constitutional challenge in 1987 (*Jones v. McKenzie*, 1987). The Fifth Circuit Court of Appeals upheld a drug-testing requirement for a custodian on the grounds that custodians operate dangerous machinery and handle toxic cleaning products and are often around students (*Aubrey v. School Board of Lafayette Parish*, 1998).

A school district's constitutional authority to require teachers to submit to suspicionless drug testing is not well established. One court ruled that teachers occupy "safety-sensitive positions" and upheld the right of a school district to require teachers to submit to a suspicionless drug test at the time of initial hiring and at the time of transfer or promotion (*Knox County Education Association v. Knox County Board of Education*, 1998). A federal court in West Virginia ruled that teachers are not safety-sensitive employees and could not be compelled to submit to random drug testing by urinalysis (*American Federation of Teachers v. Kanawha County Board of Education*, 2009).

More recently, however, a federal district court in Florida refused a plaintiff's request for an injunction against a school district that required her to submit to drug testing as a condition of employment as a substitute teacher. Although the court found that the plaintiff did not have a diminished expectation of privacy, it concluded the school district's drug-testing scheme was relatively nonintrusive. Furthermore, the school district's asserted special need to protect children under a substitute teacher's charge was "compelling indeed" (*Friedenberg v. School Board of Palm Beach County*, 2017, p. 1313).

In sum, a school district has legal authority to require school-bus drivers to submit to suspicionless drug testing along with all school employees in safety-sensitive positions, including custodians. There is no clear answer to the question of whether school districts can require teachers to submit to random, suspicionless drug testing.

The *Kanawha* case concluded they do not, while the *Friedenberg* decision ruled that school districts can at least require applicants for substitute teacher jobs to submit to drug testing as a condition of employment. In the *Knox County* case, the Sixth Circuit Court of Appeals upheld the constitutionality of a school-district policy requiring teachers to submit to drug testing at the time of initial hire and at the time of transfer or promotion. It is worth noting, however, that the drug-testing under review in that case was not conducted randomly.

Teachers' Right to Procedural Due Process prior to Termination

Tenured teachers have a property interest in continued employment and may not be terminated without being afforded procedural due process (*Board of Regents v. Roth*, 1972). In most states, school districts are required to adhere to statutory guidelines when terminating tenured teachers. Nontenured teachers have no reasonable expectation of continued employment beyond the terms of their individual contracts, and school boards may terminate nontenured teachers at the end of their contract terms without being constitutionally obligated to afford such teachers a due process hearing.

Many states, however, have laws in place governing the nonrenewal of nontenured teachers. Furthermore, public employees are entitled to a name-clearing hearing if they are terminated based on allegations that stigmatize them in their profession (*Stodghill v. Wellston School District*, 2008, p. 476).

School administrators who adhere to statutory standards when terminating a teacher will almost always be in compliance with procedural due process requirements. School authorities should also bear in mind that the Supreme Court has ruled that public employees are entitled to at least the rudiments of due process *before* they are terminated even if elaborate procedural protections are available at a post-termination hearing. The court explained that a pretermination hearing may be brief and informal and may include only an oral explanation as to why an employee is being fired (*Cleveland Board of Education v. Loudermill*, 1985).

CORPORAL PUNISHMENT AND CONSTITUTIONAL CONCERNS

Corporal punishment is either permitted or authorized by statute in twenty-two states, although its use has been declining steadily over the last thirty years. In *Ingraham v. Wright* (1977), the Supreme Court ruled that corporal punishment of students has been permitted under the common law since colonial times and that school officials can administer corporal punishment without first affording the student with a due process hearing.

The court also ruled that the corporal punishment of students does not offend the Eighth Amendment's prohibitions against cruel and unusual punishment. The Eighth Amendment, the court instructed, was meant to protect adults from "cruel and unusual" criminal punishments and had no application in the school environment.

In the wake of *Ingraham*, a number of federal appellate courts have ruled that corporal punishment that is so extreme as to be conscience-shocking infringes on a school child's liberty interest in bodily integrity and thus constitutes a violation of substantive due process under the Fourteenth Amendment (Wasserman, 2011; *Garcia v. Miera*, 1987). Among the federal circuit courts that have considered the matter, only the Fifth Circuit Court of Appeals has rejected the notion that extreme physical punishment crosses constitutional boundaries.

The Fifth Circuit (with jurisdiction over Louisiana, Mississippi, and Texas) has ruled that students have adequate civil and criminal penalties for excessive corporal punishment; and therefore, no constitutional cause of action exists regardless of the level of brutality (*Moore v. Willis Independent School District*, 2000).

CHILD-ABUSE REPORTING

All fifty states require teachers and school administrators to report suspected child abuse or neglect that they learn about in their capacity as school employees. Although the details of child-abuse statutes vary somewhat from state to state, all have these features: (1) Certain professionals (including teachers, school administrators, counselors, and child-care workers) are required by law to report any child abuse or neglect that they suspect; (2) all individuals who reported suspected child abuse or neglect in good faith are immune from civil or criminal prosecution; and (3) mandated reporters who knowingly fail to report are subject to a civil or criminal penalty.

Most school districts have child-abuse reporting policies in place that track state law, and most conduct regular training on child-abuse reporting responsibilities. Research has shown that teachers are more likely to report physical abuse when there are clear signs of injury such as burns or bruises (Stuhlmann & Fossey, 2000). They are less likely to report suspicions of sexual abuse because there are often no obvious signs.

Obviously, the decision to report involves a subjective assessment of the child's condition, and few teachers or school administrators have been prosecuted for failure to report. Nevertheless, when in doubt, it is almost always best to report the suspected abuse, and this includes suspected abuse by school employees that takes place at school. The child-abuse reporting statutes clearly place teachers and school administrators on the front lines of child-abuse detection, and all school employees should be vigilant regarding child abuse and trained in how to detect it (Fossey & Adkison, 2010).

TITLE IX: SEXUAL HARASSMENT OF STUDENTS BY PEERS OR SCHOOL EMPLOYEES

Title IX of the Education Amendments of 1972 prohibits all educational entities that receive federal funds from discriminating against employees or students based on sex. Over time, court decisions have clarified that victims of sexual harassment can sue school districts for money damages and that sexual molestation of students by teachers or other school employees constitutes a Title IX violation (*Franklin v. Gwinnett County Public Schools*, 1992). Title IX requires school districts to name a designated Title IX compliance officer and to have grievance procedures in place that victims of harassment can utilize to obtain relief.

Two important Supreme Court decisions have clarified the standards for determining when a school district is liable for sexual harassment under Title IX. In *Gebser v. Lago Vista Independent School District* (1998), the court considered a student's claim that she was sexually harassed by a teacher with whom the student had developed a sexual relationship. School officials had no knowledge of the illicit relationship and opposed the student's claim for damages under Title IX.

In *Gebser*, the Supreme Court made clear that a school district is not liable for sexual harassment by a school employee unless someone in authority knows about the harassment and responds with deliberate indifference. In *Davis v. Monroe County Board of Education* (1999), the Supreme Court clarified the standard for liability when a student is harassed by another student. The court ruled that a school district may be held liable for peer harassment when school authorities know about it and respond with deliberate indifference.

The Supreme Court also ruled that school districts are not liable under Title IX for "simple acts of teasing and name-calling among school children." To be actionable, the harassment must be "so pervasive, severe, and objectively offensive that it denies its victims the equal access to education that Title IX is designed to protect" (p. 652).

Most school districts have policies in place to ensure compliance with Title IX, and most districts offer regular training on sexual harassment and sexual discrimination. It almost goes without saying that school administrators and teachers should be proactive in preventing the development of an abusive school culture and should respond vigorously to a sexual-harassment complaint by a student or school employee.

RELIGION AND PUBLIC EDUCATION

The First Amendment to the U.S. Constitution states that Congress shall make no law "respecting an establishment of religion," and the Supreme Court has ruled that the constitutional requirement of a separation between church and state applies to all governmental units. The U.S. Supreme Court has ruled that school authorities may not sponsor prayer or Bible reading in the schools (*School District of Abington Township v. Schempp*, 1963). Nor may schools include prayer in graduation exercises (*Lee v. Weisman*, 1992) or athletic events (*Santa Fe Independent School District v. Doe*, 2000).

On the other hand, Congress passed the Equal Access Act in 1984, which requires federally funded schools to permit student-led religious groups to meet in secondary-school facilities during noninstructional time if the schools recognize any non-curriculum-related group to meet (Boy Scouts, nonvarsity athletic clubs, hobby groups, etc.). In *Board of Education of Westside Community Schools v. Mergens* (1990), the Supreme Court upheld the constitutionality of the EAA against an Establishment Clause challenge, and lower courts have ruled that the EAA requires schools to recognize gay student groups under the same terms as religious groups (*Straights and Gays for Equality v. Osseo Area Schools*, 2008).

Although the EAA, by its terms, only applies to public high schools, the Supreme Court has ruled that an elementary school must allow religious groups to its facilities during noninstructional time if it allows other civic groups to use the facilities. In *Good News Club v. Milford Central School* (2001), the court ruled that a school district had established a "limited public forum" in an elementary school by allowing various civic groups to use its facilities and was therefore obligated to allow the Good News Club, a religious group, to use its facilities on the same basis.

In *Lamb's Chapel v. Center Moriches Union Free School District* (1993), the court ruled that a New York public school district could not refuse to allow a religious group to use school facilities to show films on family life from a religious perspective. The school district allowed other civic groups to use its facilities during noninstructional time and thus was required to make those facilities available to religious groups on the same basis. The court rejected the school district's argument that it was entitled to bar access to religious groups under the Establishment Clause.

May school districts allow religious songs to be sung as part of school programs? Several courts have ruled that they may so long as religious music is interspersed with secular music and the religious music is not the basis for delivering a school-sponsored religious message. Thus, the school choir can sing "Silent Night" as part of a holiday program if it also sings "Jingle Bells" or some other secular holiday song (Cranmore & Fossey, 2014).

FAMILY EDUCATIONAL RIGHTS AND PRIVACY ACT

The Family Educational Rights and Privacy Act (FERPA), enacted by Congress in 1974, established federal standards for maintaining student records. Under FERPA, parents have a right to inspect their children's educational records and to challenge the accuracy of records on their children. In addition, school authorities must obtain parents' consent before releasing student records outside designated categories of employees who are entitled to access the records.

Most districts will have policies in place for safeguarding student records in accordance with FERPA. School officials should not worry unduly if student records are mistakenly circulated in violation of FERPA's strictures. In *Gonzaga University v. Doe* (2002), the Supreme Court ruled that FERPA does not authorize a private cause of action for damages for a FERPA violation. In fact, the only penalty for violating FERPA is loss of federal funds. So far at least, no school district has ever lost federal funding due to an inadvertent violation of FERPA.

CHAPTER SUMMARY

School leaders are required to have a working knowledge of regulatory, statutory, and constitutional law governing school operations, along with a basic understanding of their legal obligations under collective bargaining statutes and regulations. When in doubt on a particular legal issue, school administrators would be wise to consult legal counsel.

In general, education law is in harmony with basic notions of fairness. Thus, when making administrative decisions that have legal implications, school leaders should not only consult their legal counsel, they should also act in accordance with generally accepted principles of decency, fairness, and common sense.

REFERENCES

American Federation of Teachers v. Kanawha County Board of Education, 592 F. Supp. 2d 883 (S.D.W.Va. 2009).
Anderson v. Independent School District, 357 F.3d 806 (8th Cir. 2004).
Aubrey v. School Board of Lafayette Parish, 148 F.3d 559 (5th Cir. 1998).
Bethel School District No. 403 v. Fraser, 478 U.S. 675 (1986).
Board of Education of Hendrick Hudson Central School District v. Rowley, 458 U.S. 176 (1982).
Board of Education of Independent School District No. 92 of Pottawatomie County v. Earls, 536 U.S. 822 (2002).
Board of Education of Westside Community Schools v. Mergens, 496 U.S. 226 (1990).
Board of Regents of State Colleges v. Roth, 408 U.S. 564 (1972).
Brown v. Chicago Board of Education, 824 F.3d 713 (7th Cir. 2016).

Cedar Rapids Community School District v. Garret F., 526 U.S. 66 (1999).
Cleveland Board of Education v. Loudermill, 470 U.S. 532 (1985).
Cranmore, J., & Fossey, R. (2014). Religious music, the public schools, and the Establishment Clause: A review of federal case law. *Update: Applications of Research in Music Education, 33*(1), 31–35.
Davis v. Monroe County Board of Education, 526 U.S. 629 (1999).
Dixon v. Alabama State Board of Education, 294 F.2d 150 (5th Cir. 1961).
Dixon v. University of Toledo, 702 F.3d 269 (6th Cir. 2012).
Endrew F. v. Douglas County School District, 137 S. Ct. 988 (2017).
Evans-Marshall v. Tipp City Exempted Village School District, 624 F.3d 332 (6th Cir. 2010).
Fossey, R., & Adkison, J. (2010). Molestation and rumors of molestation: Educators can do more to stop sexual abuse in schools. *Teachers College Record Online*, tcrecord.org. ID Number 16252.
Franklin v. Gwinnett County Public Schools, 503 U.S. 60 (1992).
Friedenberg v. School Board of Palm Beach County, 257 F. Supp. 3d 1295 (S.D. Fla. 2017).
Garcetti v. Ceballos, 126 S.Ct. 1951 (2006).
Garcia v. Miera, 817 F.2d 650 (10th Cir. 1987).
Gebser v. Lago Vista Independent School District, 524 U.S. 274 (1998).
Gonzaga University v. Doe, 536 U.S. 273 (2002).
Good News Club v. Milford Central School, 533 U.S. 98 (2001).
Goss v. Lopez, 419 U.S. 565 (1975).
Hazelwood School District v. Kuhlmeier, 484 U.S. 260 (1988).
Ingraham v. Wright, 430 U.S. 651 (1977).
Irving Independent School District v. Tatro, 468 U.S. 883 (1984).
Jones v. McKenzie, 833 F.2d 335 (D.C. Cir. 1987).
Khachatourian v. Hacienda La Puente Unified School District, 572 Fed. Appx. 556 (9th Cir. 2014).
Kinsey v. Salado Independent School District, 950 F.2d 988 (5th Cir. 1992).
Knox County Education Association v. Knox County Board of Education, 158 F.3d 361 (6th Cir. 1998).
Kowalski v. Berkeley County Schools, 652 F.3d 565 (4th Cir. 2011).
Lamb's Chapel v. Center Moriches Union Free School District, 508 U.S. 384 (1993).
Lee v. Weisman, 505 U.S. 577 (1992).
Miles v. Denver Public Schools, 944 F.2d 773 (10th Cir. 1991).
Moore v. Willis Independent School District, 233 F.3d 871 (5th Cir. 2000).
Morse v. Frederick, 551 U.S. 393 (2007).
New Jersey v. TLO, 469 U.S. 325 (1985).
Pickering v. Board of Education, 391 U.S. 563 (1968).
Safford Unified School District v. Redding, 557 U.S. 364 (2009).
Santa Fe Independent School District v. Doe, 530 U.S. 290 (2000).
School District of Abington Township v. Schempp and Murray v. Curlett, 324 U.S. 203 (1963).
Shaul v. Cherry Valley–Springfield Central School District, 363 F.3d 177 (2nd Cir. 2004).
Stodghill v. Wellston School District, 512 F.3d 472 (8th Cir. 2008).
Straights and Gays for Equality v. Osseo Area Schools, 540 F.3d 911 (8th Cir. 2008).
Stuhlmann, J., & Fossey, R. (2000). Child abuse: What teachers in the 90s know, think, and do. *Journal of Education for Students Placed at Risk, 5*(3), 251–266.
Veronia School District 47J v. Acton, 515 U.S. 646 (1995).
Wasserman, L. (2011). Corporal punishment in K–12 settings: Reconsideration of its constitutional dimensions thirty years after *Ingraham v. Wright*. *Touro Law Review, 26,* 1029–1101.
Williams v. Dallas Independent School District, 480 F.2d 689 (5th Cir. 2007).

Index

abuse. *See* child-abuse reporting
accountability, 1–5, 9, 60–61
activities: extracurricular, 62, 67; physical, 4; strategies and, 34–35
adequate yearly progress (AYP) goals, 9
administrators. *See* school employees; teachers
advances, medical, 41–42
affective domain, 3–4
agent, change, 41–42
alignment. *See* systems alignment
American Federation of Teachers v. Kanawha County Board of Education (2009), 81
analogy, for SIP, 10–11
analysis: financial needs, 61; root cause analysis (RCA), 8, 12, 13
analysis, data, 25, 27, 29; for schools, 8, 9, 23–24; for SIP, 8–9, 11–12
assessment, needs, 33–34
AYP. *See* adequate yearly progress

Bamburg, Jerry D., 26
Bandura, Albert, 47
behavior, student, xiii
beliefs: school vision and, 21–23, 28, 29; of stakeholders, 29
Bethel School District v. Fraser (1986), 72
Brown v. Chicago Board of Education (2016), 77–78
bullying, 73

bus drivers, 81

case studies, 44, 46, 50–52, 53–54
Center on Educational Governance, 25
challenges: educational, xiii–xiv; overcoming, 53–54
change, 36, 42; collective efficacy and, 47–48; of district policies, 59; first-order, 42; initiating, 48–50; leadership and, 56; Managing Complex Change Model, 54; mandates for, 55; process of, 48, 54–56; readiness for, 43–44, 55; resistance to, 55; school leaders and, 48, 51; second-order, 42–43, 51; stages of, 43, 51, 52–53; understanding, 42–43; vision for, 48–49. *See also* reform
change agent, 41; principal as, 41–42
characteristics, of SIP, 15–17
checks, routine, 52
child-abuse reporting, 83
climate. *See* school climate
climate and culture data, 24
cognitive domain, 3–4
collective efficacy, 47, 51; change and, 47–48
college, 4–5; admission to, 9; credits for, 60, 61
committee, for communication plan, 33
communication: community, 37; methods of, 37; negative, 37, 38; school-to-

home, 37, 38
communication plan, 31–32, 34, 39; committee for, 33; contextual design of, 32–33; evaluation of, 36; monitoring for, 35–36; stakeholders and, 33; strategies for, 34–35; survey for, 37; timeline for, 35
community: communication with, 37; engagement with, 31–39; support from, 50
community, and school, 27, 31–33, 39; partnership of, 36–37; stakeholder perceptions of, 39
community business connections, 38
community stakeholders, 31, 32
Conant, James B., 4
connections: community business, 38; with parents, 37
consensus statement, 28
Constitution, US: Eighth Amendment, 82; First Amendment, 72, 77, 78, 79, 85; Fourteenth Amendment, 82; Fourth Amendment, 80
constitutional rights: concerns for, 82–83; of school employees, 76–82; student, 71, 72–76; teacher, 71, 79–82
contextual design, of communication plan, 32–33
corporal punishment, 72, 82–83
credits, college, 60, 61
crisis management team, 34–35
culture. *See* school culture
curriculum, 4–5
custodians, 81

data: analysis of, 8–9, 11–12, 23–24, 25, 27, 29; climate and culture, 24; demographic, 25; end-of-year, 8, 9; evaluation of school, 8, 9; from needs assessment, 34; perceptions of stakeholders, 39; performance, 24, 25; types of, 8
data team, 23–24, 26; organization and actions of, 24–25
Davis v. Monroe County Board of Education (1999), 84
demarginalization, 1–2; equality and, 2
democratic society, 2, 5
demographics, 32–33; data for, 25; student, xiii
design, contextual, 32–33
development: of human being, 3–4; socioemotional, 4
differentiated instruction, 3–4, 5
disabled students, 67
discipline, physical, 72
discussion, of systems alignment, 66–68
district policies, 58; changing, 59; dissecting, 60–61; impact of, 61–62; systems alignment to, 59–60
Dixon v. University of Toledo (2012), 78
domains: affective, 3–4, 5; cognitive, 3–4, 5; integration of, 4–5; psychomotor, 3–4, 5
drug tests, 73–74, 81–82
due process, procedural, 74, 76, 82

EAA. *See* Equal Access Act
efficacy, 52; collective, 47–48, 51; self-, 46–47; teacher, 46–48, 51
Eighth Amendment, US Constitution, 82
emergencies, 34–35
employees. *See* school employees
end-of-year data, 8, 9
engagement, community, 31–39
Equal Access Act (EAA) (1984), 85
equality, 2–3, 5, 84; demarginalization and, 2; EAA and, 85; teachers and, 49. *See also* inequality
evaluation: communication plan, 36; of implementation plan, 63–64; of school data, 8, 9; of staff, 7
experiences: mastery, 47, 51; vicarious, 47
expulsion and suspension, 74
extracurricular activities, 62, 67

faculty leadership team, 48–49; teachers and, 49
Family Educational Rights and Privacy Act (FERPA) (1974), 72, 86
finances, 66–67
financial needs analysis, 61
Fiore, Douglas, 45
First Amendment, US Constitution, 72, 77, 78, 79, 85
first-order change, 42
food services, 38, 68

format, for SIP, 17–18
Fourteenth Amendment, US Constitution, 82
Fourth Amendment, US Constitution, 80
freedom, 2; to learn, 3; from searches and seizures, 73–74, 76, 79–82
free speech, 72–73, 76–79
Friedenberg v. School Board of Palm Beach County (2017), 81
funding, xiii, 44, 49, 63
future, of schools, 23

Garcetti v. Ceballos (2006), 77
Gebser v. Lago Vista Independent School District (1998), 84
goals, 13; AYP, 9; of schools, 7, 10, 26, 32; setting, 27–28, 34; short-term, 43; for SIP, 13; stakeholders and, 26–28
governance structure, of school, 21
graduates, 29
grants, 44; writing, 66–67

harassment, sexual, 84
Hazelwood School District v. Kuhlmeier (1988), 72
home environment, of students, xiii
human being, development of, 3–4
human resources, xiii, 67
hypothesis, for SIP, 12–13

iceberg metaphor, 45
IDEIA. *See* Individuals with Disabilities Education Improvement Act
impact, of district policies, 61–62
implementation, of reform, 50–52
implementation, stage of change, 43
implementation plan, 59–60; creating, 62–63; evaluating, 63–64; monitoring, 63; Plains School District, 61–62; refining, 63
Individuals with Disabilities Education Improvement Act (IDEIA) (2004), 71, 75–76
inequality, 1, 2
influence, of school leaders, 26
infrastructure, of injustice, 2
Ingraham v. Wright (1977), 82
initiation, stage of change, 43, 51
injustice, infrastructure of, 2

instruction, differentiated, 3–4, 5
Instructional Leadership (Del Favero), xiv
integration, of domains, 4–5
intervention: SIP strategies for, 8, 14. *See also* Response to Intervention

Mr. Jones (assistant principal), 62–63
justice, xiv; principles of, 1, 2–5; social, 1–2

Kinsey v. Salado Independent School District (1992), 78

Lamb's Chapel v. Center Moriches Union Free School District (1993), 85
laws, 58, 71, 86; systems alignment to, 58–59, 68. *See also* constitutional rights
leaders. *See* school leaders
leadership, 26; change and, 56; faculty leadership team, 48–49; school culture and, 46; vision-based, 26
learning environments, student-centered, 53–54
Leithwood, Kenneth, 26
liberties, student, 3
low-performing schools, 44

Managing Complex Change Model, 54
mandates: for change, 55; NCLB, 58–59
marginalization, 2
Marzano, Robert, 42–43
mastery experiences, 47, 51
math, 12
medical advances, 41–42
metaphor: iceberg, 45; science experiment, 43–44
methods, of communication, 37
micomanagement, 54
mission statement, 21–22, 23, 65–66. *See also* school mission
monitoring: for communication plan, 35–36; implementation plan, 63; of SIP, 14–15; timeline for, 36
moral purpose, 48, 55
Morse v. Frederick (2007), 72
Mt. Healthy City School District v. Doyle (1977), 78–79
music, religious, 85–86

National Study of School Evaluation (NSSE), 28–29
NCLB. *See* No Child Left Behind Act
needs, of students, xiv, 7–8
needs assessment, 33; data from, 34
negative communication, 37, 38
New Jersey v. TLO (1985), 73
No Child Left Behind Act (NCLB) (2002), 9; mandates from, 58–59
NSSE. *See* National Study of School Evaluation

organization and actions, data team, 24–25
overcoming challenges, 53–54

parents, connections with, 37
partnership, of community and school, 36–37
perceptions, of stakeholders, 39
performance, student, 27, 28
performance data, 24, 25
persuasion, verbal, 47
pet projects, 63–64
phone calls, 35
physical activity, 4
physical discipline, 72
Pickering v. Board of Education (1968), 76–77
Plains School District, 60, 62–64; implementation plan for, 61–62; statements for, 64; system alignment for, 66–68
plan. *See* communication plan; implementation plan; school improvement plan (SIP)
PLC. *See* professional learning community
policies. *See* district policies
poverty, xiii
prayer, 72
principals, xiii, 5, 41, 49, 53–54, 55; as change agents, 41–42; SIP and, 10–11, 18
principles, of justice, 1; Rawl's, 2–5
privilege, 1
proactiveness, 34, 35
procedural due process, 74, 76, 82
process: change, 48, 54–56; SIP, 11–13
professional learning community (PLC), 44

psychomotor domains, 3–4
punishment, corporal, 72, 82–83
purpose: moral, 48, 55; of school, 32

Rawls, John, 2–5
RCA. *See* root cause analysis
readiness: for change, 43–44, 55; for reform, 44–45
records, student, 86
reevaluation, of reform, 52–53
reform, 44; implementing, 50–52; readiness for, 44–45; reevaluating, 52–53; teachers and, 51–52
Reform Readiness Survey, 48
relationships, 36
religion, 72, 85–86
religious music, 85–86
reporting child-abuse, 83
resistance, to change, 55
resources, 51; human, xiii, 67
Response to Intervention, 50
revision, of school vision, 28–29
rights. *See* constitutional rights
role, of teachers, 38
root cause analysis (RCA), 8, 12, 13
routine checks, 52

school climate, 64; school culture versus, 45–46
school community, values of, 22, 28
school culture, 26, 44, 64; leadership and, 46; school climate versus, 45–46
school employees: constitutional rights of, 76–82; termination of, 78–79, 82. *See also* faculty leadership team; teachers
school improvement plan (SIP), 7–19, 16; analogy for, 10–11; characteristics of, 15–17; data analysis for, 8–9, 11–12; as dynamic, 15–17; format for, 17–18; goals for, 13, 26; hypothesis for, 12–13; intervention strategies for, 8, 14; monitoring of, 14–15; principals and, 10–11, 18; process of, 11–13; school vision as basis for, 11; team for, 8, 9, 18–19; templates for, 17–18
school improvement strategies, 7, 12–13; monitoring, 14
school leaders: change and, 48, 51; influence of, 26; school vision and,

23–24
school mission, 32; statement for, 21–22, 23, 65–66; systems alignment and, 64–65, 68
schools: communication plan for, 31–32, 32; community and, 27, 31–33, 36–37, 39; data analysis of, 8, 9; future of, 23; goals of, 7, 10, 32; governance structure of, 21; low-performing schools, 44; purpose of, 32
school-to-home communications, 37, 38
school vision, 10, 21, 23, 26, 29, 32; beliefs and, 21–23, 28, 29; new, 28–29; revised, 28–29; school leaders and, 23–24; SIP based on, 11; statement for, 21–23, 29, 64, 65–66; systems alignment and, 64–65, 68
school walk-throughs, 14
science experiment metaphor, 43–44
searches and seizures, freedom from, 73–74, 76, 79–82
second-order change, 42–43, 51
segregation, of students, 4–5
self-efficacy, 46–47
setting goals, 27–28, 34
sexual harassment, of students, 84
Shaul v. Cherry Valley–Springfield Central School District (2004), 80
short-term goals, 43
Dr. Simpson (superintendent), 66
SIP. *See* school improvement plan
SIP team, 8, 9, 18–19
skills, team-building, 27
Mrs. Smith (career director), 62, 63
social justice, 1–2
social media, 73
society, 38; democratic, 2
socioemotional development, 4
special education, 67, 75–76
staff, evaluation of, 7
stages, of change, 43, 51, 52–53
stakeholders, 7, 11, 13; beliefs of, 29; communication plan and, 33; community, 31, 32; goals and, 26–28; perceptions of, 39
statements, 65; consensus, 28; mission, 21–22, 23, 65–66, 66; for Plains School District, 64; vision, 21–23, 29, 64, 65–66

strategies: activities and, 34–35; for communication plan, 34–35; for school improvement, 7, 12–13, 14; for SIP intervention, 8, 14
strengths, 25–26, 27
student-centered learning environments, 53–54
student performance, 27, 28
students: behavior of, xiii; of color, 1; constitutional rights of, 71, 72–76; demographics of, xiii; disabled, 67; home environment of, xiii; liberties of, 3; needs of, xiv, 7–8; records of, 86; segregation of, 4–5; sexual harassment of, 84
Sun, Jingping, 26
support, community, 50
Supreme Court, US, 74, 76–77, 79, 85
survey: for communication plan, 37; Reform Readiness Survey, 48
suspension and expulsion, 74
sustainability, stage of change, 43, 52–53
systems: teacher evaluation, 46; teacher improvement, 44
systems alignment, 58; discussion of, 66–68; to district policies, 59–60; to laws, 58–59, 68; mission and vision and, 64–66, 68; for Plains School District, 66–68

teacher efficacy, 46–48, 51
teacher evaluation system, 46
teacher handbook, 41
teacher improvement system, 44
teachers, xiii; equality and, 49; faculty leadership team and, 49; reform and, 51–52; rights of, 71, 79–82; role of, 38
team: crisis management, 34–35; data, 23–25, 26; faculty leadership, 48–49; SIP, 8, 9, 18–19
team-building skills, 27
technology, 31, 34
templates, for SIP, 17–18
termination, of school employees, 78–79, 82
tests, drug, 73–74, 81–82
text messages, 35
theory, Rawl's, 2
A Theory of Justice (Rawls), 2–5

timeline: for communication plan, 35; for monitoring, 36
Tinker v. Des Moines Community School District (1971), 72
Title funds, 44
Title IX, Education Amendment (1972), 84
Tomlinson, Carol Ann, 3
traditions, 45
transportation, 68
types, of data, 8

understanding change, 42–43
United States (US): Constitution, 72, 77, 78, 79, 80, 82, 84, 85; Supreme Court, 74, 76–77, 79, 85; Title IX, Education Amendment, 84
University of Louisiana, xvi

University of Southern California, 25
US. *See* United States

values, of school community, 22, 28
verbal persuasion, 47
Vernonia School District 437J v. Acton (1995), 74
vicarious experiences, 47
vision, for change, 48–49
vision-based leadership, 26
vision statement, 21–23, 29, 64, 65–66. *See also* school vision
vocational education, 4–5

walk-throughs, school, 14
website, school, 57–58
writing grants, 66–67

About the Editor and Contributors

Frank S. Del Favero holds the title of professor in the Educational Foundations and Leadership Department in the College of Education at the University of Louisiana at Lafayette. He holds a certificate of advanced study in educational administration and a PhD degree specializing in educational administration and policy studies from SUNY Albany. He teaches educational leadership courses at the graduate level involving the use of data to effect change, the evaluation of effective assessments and instructional strategies, and school vision. His approach to teaching at the postsecondary level integrates academic theory with his extensive background as a K–12 education practitioner.

* * *

Dr. Nancy P. Autin is an associate professor at the University of Louisiana at Lafayette. She teaches graduate and undergraduate courses in the Department of Educational Foundations and Leadership. Dr. Autin earned her PhD from the University of New Orleans in curriculum and instruction with an emphasis in mathematics. Prior to teaching at the university, Dr. Autin served in various capacities in K–12 education: principal, academic assistant principal, supervisor of instruction, Mathematics Department chair, and classroom teacher. As a school administrator, Dr. Autin initiated programs and conducted workshops for school administrators and teachers including analyzing school data, designing a school vision, monitoring and evaluating instruction and the curriculum, improving instructional and assessment practices, and customizing professional growth opportunities for all levels of experience. Dr. Autin taught high school mathematics courses at all levels, from Algebra I to Advanced Placement Calculus. At the University of Louisiana at Lafayette, Dr. Autin serves on several committees including Faculty Senate, Student Evaluation of Instruction, Academic Planning, Masters in Educational Leadership, Grade Appeals, College of Education Honors Program, and College of Education Commencement Committee. She serves as lead evaluator for schools seeking accreditation through AdvancED. Dr. Autin is vice president and chair of the board of directors of a nonprofit, Raphael-Evelyn Education Foundation, whose mission is to establish schools in Nigeria with a focus on developing leadership and technology skills to advance self-governance and self-reliance in communities throughout Nigeria.

Tarrah C. Davis is an associate professor at the University of Louisiana at Lafayette in the College of Education and Department of Educational Foundations and Leadership. She holds an EdD degree in educational leadership. Her teaching career in K–12 education spans nine years where she served the gifted and talented student population. She currently works in the university's College of Education as assessment coordinator and currently teaches courses at both the undergraduate and graduate levels.

Richard Fossey is the Paul Burdin Endowed Professor of Education at the University of Louisiana at Lafayette. He received his JD degree from the University of Texas School of Law and his doctorate in education policy from Harvard Graduate School of Education. He has written extensively on education law and policy issues and serves on the Editorial Advisory Board of Education Law Reporter and Teachers College Record .

Amanda Shuford Mayeaux is an assistant professor in the Department of Educational Foundations and Leadership at the University of Louisiana at Lafayette. As an educator for more than twenty-five years, she has worked in a variety of campuses spanning grades Pre-K through 12 in a variety of contexts from teacher to administration. Dr. Mayeaux has won several national teaching awards, including the Milken Educator Award in 2003 and Disney's Outstanding Teacher of the Year in 2006, along with her teaching team partners, Monique Wild and Kathryn Edmonds. Her research interests are expert teachers, motivation factors, professional learning, change process, school culture, and effective leadership.

Nathan M. Roberts is the dean of the College of Education at the University of Louisiana at Lafayette. He earned both his law degree and his PhD from Louisiana State University. Nathan is a former school board attorney who teaches master's and doctoral courses in school law, organizing the learning environment and legal liability in tourism and sports and recreation. His research focuses on legal issues that affect educational leaders. He served as the chair of the educational leadership program redesign for the college and on the EdD design team with UL Lafayette. He is a Louisiana mediator for special education cases and a former due process hearing officer. He is also a founding board member of the nonprofit National SAM Innovation Project that operates in more than seven hundred schools in twenty-two states.

Robert O. Slater holds a PhD in education policy from the University of Chicago and a master's degree in the same field from Harvard University. Before coming to the University of Louisiana in 2007, he was a professor at Texas A&M University (seventeen years), at Louisiana State University (two years), and the University of Maryland (five years). Prior to becoming department head, he served as coordinator of the College of Education's only doctoral program, which has more than one hundred active students. Dr. Slater has published two books, a monograph, and numerous articles on the effects of education on American society and democracy. He has been selected three times as a Fulbright Scholar, to Peru (1996), Bolivia (2010), and most recently to Greece (2018). Dr. Slater's current interests focus on the implications of John Rawls's *Theory of Justice* for K–12 education.

Erin Stokes, EdD, is the principal at Pineville Elementary School in Louisiana and has served as an adjunct professor at Louisiana College and at the University of Louisiana at Lafayette in its MEd program in educational leadership. Her research interests include the effects of school culture, climate, and collective efficacy on school reform. In 2017, she won the Louisiana Educational Research Association Award for Outstanding Research, and she presented her research at the American Educational Research Association Conference in San Antonio and New York City and the Visible Learning Conference in San Francisco.

www.ingramcontent.com/pod-product-compliance
Lightning Source LLC
Chambersburg PA
CBHW032030230426
43671CB00005B/261